Louis Albert Banks

White Slaves

Or, the oppression of the worthy poor

Louis Albert Banks

White Slaves
Or, the oppression of the worthy poor

ISBN/EAN: 9783744797467

Printed in Europe, USA, Canada, Australia, Japan

Cover: Foto ©ninafisch / pixelio.de

More available books at **www.hansebooks.com**

Sincerely Yours
Louis Albert Banks

OR

THE OPPRESSION OF THE WORTHY POOR

BY

REV. LOUIS ALBERT BANKS, D.D.
AUTHOR OF "THE PEOPLE'S CHRIST," ETC.

BOSTON
LEE AND SHEPARD PUBLISHERS
10 MILK STREET
1893

COPYRIGHT, 1891, BY LEE AND SHEPARD

All Rights Reserved

WHITE SLAVES

PRESS OF
Rockwell and Churchill,
BOSTON.

TO

My Father and Mother,

WHO INSTILLED INTO MY MIND AND HEART, IN THE DAYS OF
A HAPPY BOYHOOD, THEIR OWN LOVE FOR LIBERTY
AND HATRED OF OPPRESSION,

THIS VOLUME IS GRATEFULLY DEDICATED.

To the Mercy and Help Department of the Epworth League

Mr. Edison tells us that ninety per cent of the energy that there is in coal is lost in the present method of converting it into a usable force. May I, without being considered a croaker, say that almost the same amount of spiritual power goes to waste in our average church life? One is startled at times as he notes the manifestations of fervor and warmth in the devotional meetings of the present day, and the meagre results that follow in the transformation of society into the likeness of the kingdom of heaven. Exactly what we have to do, however, is to help hasten the answer to the prayer our Lord taught us, "Thy will be done on earth as it is in heaven," and not to be forever seeking to build tabernacles on some Mount of Transfiguration.

This book of Dr. Banks's is a positive stimulus to this work of social transformation. The young men and women of our Epworth League could not do better than to carefully and thoughtfully study its vivid pictures of every-day scenes in our great, and even in our lesser, cities.

Such study will open their eyes to sad deformities in their own communities, to which too many have become strangely indifferent through custom and wont. True, it is not pleasant to consider these distressing matters; but is it the business of the Christian to avoid that which is unpleasant? Consideration leads to sympathy, and sympathy wonderfully quickens the inventive faculties; and the aroused intellect and active affection are leavening forces that alter social conditions always for the better.

I take great pleasure, therefore, in commending this work, because it stirs all who read it. It may make you indignant. What of it? Would that more were alive enough to be indignant with the indignation of our Lord at the forces of unbrotherliness at work in our midst! It will do more than rouse your indignation; it will help you to utter the prayer that gave the accent to the life of Paul: "Lord, what wilt thou have *me* to do?" When in works of Mercy and Help our tens of thousands of Epworth Leaguers are loyally living this prayer, the problem of Edison, as applied to spiritual dynamics, will be solved, and the latent forces of spiritual energy used to their utmost. Then, as slavery has passed away, war and tyranny and idleness and poverty will be no more, and the end to which Christ leads us, and for which He died, will be attained.

WILLIAM INGRAHAM HAVEN,

Vice-President for Mercy and Help Department.

INWOOD LODGE, PINE ISLAND N.H.
August 1893

AUTHOR'S PREFACE

THIS volume had its origin in experiences which came to me in the daily duties of a city pastorate. The inadequate wages received by some of the members of my own congregation, and the impoverished and unhealthy surroundings of many of the poor people who came for me to christen their children, pray with their sick, or bury their dead, so aroused my sympathy for the victims, and my indignation against the cruel or indifferent causes of their misery, that I determined upon a thorough and systematic investigation of the conditions of life among the worthy Boston poor. By the word "worthy" I do not mean to indicate a class of saints, but the poor people of the city who are willing and anxious to exchange honest hard work for their support. I have not, in the series of studies here presented, entered into a discussion of the vicious and criminal classes. I have tried to perform, as it seemed to me, a far more important task — to make a plea for justice on behalf of the crushed, and often forgotten, victims of greed, who work and starve in their cellars and garrets rather than beg or steal.

The larger part of the matter contained in these pages was originally delivered in a series of discourses from the pulpit of St. John's Methodist Episcopal Church, South Boston, and retains here the direct form of the spoken address.

I desire to make a personal acknowledgment to some who have given me great assistance in making the investigations, the results of which are here recorded. I am greatly indebted to Mr. B. O. Flower, Editor of *The Arena*, for many kindnesses, and especially for the use of several interesting illustrations originally prepared for the magazine over which he so ably and gracefully presides. The Rev. Walter J. Swaffield, of the Boston Baptist Bethel, the Rev. C. L. D. Younkin, of the North End Mission, the Rev. Geo. L. Small, of the Mariners'

House, the Rev. John G. May, of the Italian Mission, and that indefatigable reformer, Mrs. Alice N. Lincoln, have each put me under great obligations by their unwearying kindness and willing assistance. I am also greatly indebted to Mr. Sears Gallagher, the brilliant young South Boston artist, and to the veteran photographer of Boston Highlands, Mr. W. H. Partridge, for many courtesies in connection with the illustrations which illumine these chapters.

Louis Albert Banks.

Boston, *September* 15, 1891.

CONTENTS

		PAGE
I.	THE WHITE SLAVES OF THE BOSTON "SWEATERS"	17
II.	LETTER OF CRITICISM	47
III.	REPLY TO A CRITICISM ON "THE WHITE SLAVES OF THE BOSTON SWEATERS"	55
IV.	THE PLAGUE OF THE SWEAT-SHOP	81
V.	THE RELATION OF WAGES TO MORALS	109
VI.	THE WAGES AND TEMPTATIONS OF WORKING-PEOPLE	137
VII.	BOSTON'S UNCLE TOM'S CABIN	145
VIII.	SOCIAL MICROBES IN BOSTON TENEMENT HOUSES, AND HOW TO DESTROY THEM	179
IX.	OLD WORLD TIDES IN BOSTON	213
X.	OUR BROTHERS AND SISTERS, THE BOSTON PAUPERS	257
XI.	COMMENT ON "OUR BROTHERS AND SISTERS, THE BOSTON PAUPERS"	283
XII.	THE GOLD GOD OF MODERN SOCIETY	305

LIST OF ILLUSTRATIONS

	PAGE
Portrait of Author	*Frontispiece*
Portuguese Widow in Attic	21
Portuguese Widow and Children	29
Little Children Finishing Pants	31
Invalid in Chair	33
Postal Uniforms	37
A Tenement-house Court	58
Sunday on North Street	64
Clark's Mission	70
North End Junk Shop	74
Home of the Mathers	77
The Peanutter	85
Inside a Sweat-shop	92
Paul Revere House, North Square	98
Rear of North End Tenement House	102
Commonwealth Avenue	104
Drying "The Find"	111
The North End Mission	116
A Boston "Bridge of Sighs"	128
Court Off North Street	148
Cellarway Leading to Underground Apartments	151
Sick Man in Underground Apartment	155
An Ancient Tenement	160
Italian Fruit-venders at Home	163
Cockroaches by Flash-light	165
Banana Seller	166
Underground Tenement with Two Beds	169
Two O'clock in the Morning	175

LIST OF ILLUSTRATIONS

	PAGE
EXTERIOR OF A NORTH END TENEMENT HOUSE	183
WIDOW AND TWO CHILDREN IN UNDERGROUND TENEMENT	187
THE BANK OF THE UNFORTUNATE	193
OUT OF WORK	195
A CHEAP LODGING-HOUSE	199
THE "GOOD LUCK" TENEMENT HOUSE	206
THE SAND GARDEN	209
CHRIST CHURCH TOWER	215
ON THE CUNARDER	219
ON THE WAY TO THE RABBI	221
PASSING THE QUARANTINE DOCTOR	224
SURGICAL THEOLOGY	229
BUILDING USED BY THE BRITISH AS A HOSPITAL	232
VICTORIA SQUARE	235
OAK DOOR AT ENTRANCE	238
READING-ROOM AT FACTORY	241
FERRIS BROTHERS' CORSET FACTORY	247
QUARTER SECTION OF ONE OF THE WORK ROOMS	244
THE QUEEN OF THE DUMP	252
TRAMPS	261
WOMEN'S HOSPITAL WARD AT LONG ISLAND	284
GETTING A BREATH OF FRESH AIR	289
ATTIC AT RAINSFORD ISLAND	295
MARINERS' HOME	298
CHILDREN PLAYING IN COPP'S HILL BURYING-GROUND	309
DIGGING IN THE ASH-BARRELS IN WINTER	312
FOUR SHINERS	314
SOUTH BOSTON RAG-PICKERS	317

I

THE WHITE SLAVES OF THE BOSTON "SWEATERS"

"Hard work is good an' wholesome, past all doubt;
But 'tain't so, ef the mind gits tuckered out."

JAMES RUSSELL LOWELL: *Biglow Papers.*

WHITE SLAVES

I

THE WHITE SLAVES OF THE BOSTON "SWEATERS"

A WISE man of the old time, after a tour of observation, came home to say, "So I returned, and considered all the oppressions that are done under the sun: and behold the tears of such as were oppressed, and they had no comforter; and on the side of their oppressors there was power; but they had no comforter." If this report had been written by one who had been climbing with me through the tenement houses of not less than a score of Boston streets, conversing with the sewing-women, looking on their poverty-lined faces and their ragged children, breathing the poisonous air of the quarters where they work, and listening to their heart-rending stories of cruelty and oppression, it would be an appropriate summary of our observation. It is my purpose, at this time, to take you with me on a tour of observation. As well-lighted streets are better than policemen to insure safety and good order, so I believe that the best possible service I can render the public is to turn on the light, and tell, as plainly and simply as I can, the story of what I have seen and heard and smelled in the white slave-quarters, which are a disgrace to our fair city.

I shall confine myself at this time entirely to the work of women and children in their own homes. Most of this work is parcelled out to them by middlemen who are known as "sweaters." That word sweater is not in the old dictionaries. It is a foul word, born of the greed and infernal lust for gold which pervade the most reckless and wicked financial circles of our time. The sweater takes large contracts and divides it out among the very poor, reducing the price to starvation limits, and reserving the profits for himself.

Some of the women whose story I shall tell do not work for sweaters, but are treated almost as badly by the powerful and wealthy firms who employ them. In these cases the firm itself has learned the sweater's secret, and through an agent of its own is sweating the life-blood out of these half-starved victims.

Let us begin near at home with a South Boston case, which came to my notice through the dispensary doctor for the district. It is a widow with one child — a little boy scarcely three years old. The child is just recovering from a troublesome sickness, through which the doctor became acquainted with her. She has been sewing for a good while for one of the largest and most respectable dry-goods houses on Washington Street — a firm whose name is a household word throughout New England. Her sewing has been confined to two lines — cloaks and aprons. For some time she has been making white aprons — a good long apron, requiring a yard, perhaps, of material; it is hemmed across the bottom and on both sides, the band or "apron string" is hemmed on both sides, and then sewed on to the apron, making six long seams. For these she is paid fifteen cents *a dozen!* And besides that, this great, rich firm, whose members are rolling in wealth and luxury, charges this poor widow fifteen cents expressage on her package of ten dozen aprons, so that for making one hundred and twenty aprons, such as I have described, she receives, net, one hundred and thirty-five cents! If she works from seven o'clock in the morning until eleven o'clock at night, she can make four dozen; but, with the care of her child, she is unable to average more than three dozen, for which, after the expressage is taken out, she receives forty cents a day for the support of herself and child.

Her rent for the one little room is one dollar per week. It is idle to say that this firm is compelled to do this by competition, for the material and making of these aprons cost less than ten cents, and the firm retails them ordinarily at *twenty-five cents apiece*. On cloaks she did better, receiving from fifty to seventy-five cents apiece, she furnishing her own sewing-silk and cotton. On these she could make, by working from seven A. M. till eleven P. M., nearly a dollar a day, but she could never get more than six cloaks a week, so that the income for the week was about the same.

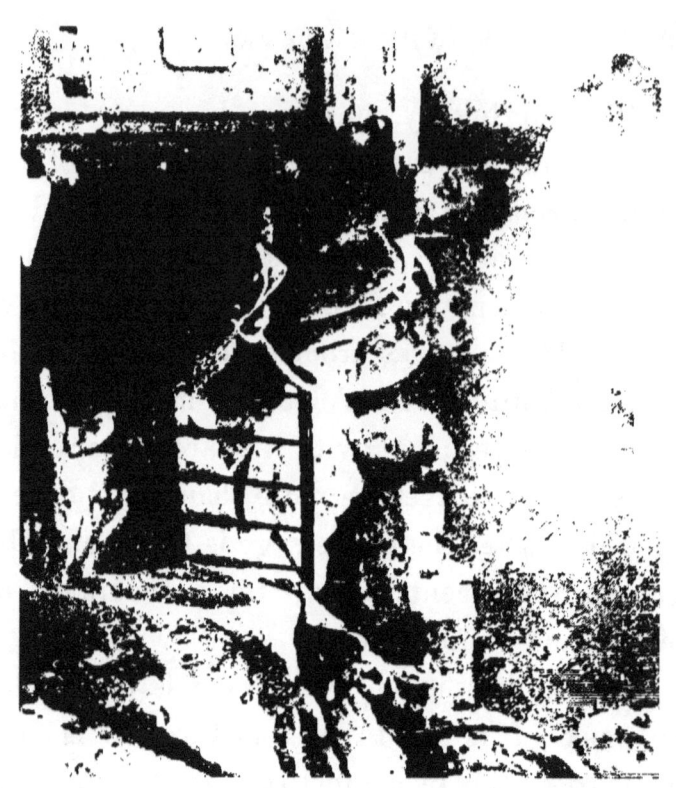

Now come with me a little farther around the harbor. Let us climb up three flights, to a little attic suite of two rooms, so low at the side that, with my length of anatomy, I have to keep well to the middle of the room in order to stand upright. Here live a Portuguese mother and five children, the oldest thirteen, the youngest not yet three, a poor, deformed, little thing that has consumption of the bowels, brought on by scanty and irregular food. Its tiny legs are scarcely thicker than my thumb, and you cannot look at its patient, wasted, little face, that looks old enough to have endured twenty-five years of misery, instead of three, without the heartache. I ask the mother how she earns her living, and she points to a package that has just come in. Picking it up, and untying the strings, I find there six pairs of pants, cut out and basted up, ready for making. Looking at the card, we are astonished to find that it bears the name of one of the largest firms in the city of Boston, a firm known, perhaps, as widely as any. Three pairs of these pants are *custom-made;* they are fashionable summer trousers, with the names and addresses of the men for whom they are made tacked on them. The other three pairs are stamped with "New York" as customer, from which we infer that they are made for a New York house, the Boston firm acting as sweater. This woman and her little children must finish these pants by the same hour tomorrow, when the messenger from the store will bring a new lot and take these away. She receives *ten cents a pair* — three pairs being *custom-made* pants! In order to finish the six pairs in the twenty-four hours, she must get to work at six in the morning, and improve every available moment until eleven or twelve in the evening, and sometimes, if the sick child is fretful, until one o'clock in the morning. Her wages for this tremendous strain that is wearing her very life away, until she looks almost as frail as her dying child, is *sixty cents!* Her rent for these two small attic pockets is one dollar and fifty cents per week. She has one bed for herself and five children. Only through the aid of the Boston Baptist Bethel is she able to keep up the struggle. And yet, O my brothers! this is in sight of the old North Church, and the tower where they hung the lanterns for a signal to Paul Revere, when he rode through the darkness to arouse the Fathers to fight against oppression. God help us to hang another light for liberty in the midst of this cruel slavery!

Perhaps you are tired now, and want to rest, but I am insatiable, and will go on. Let me give you the record of six families found in the same tenement.

Family No. 1. They are Italians. The wife and mother is finishing cheap overcoats at four cents apiece. She can finish from eight to ten in a day. She has two finer coats, lined with handsome satin; of these she can complete only five a day, and receives eight cents apiece. There are three in the family, and they pay a dollar and a half per week for their one room. I asked about the husband, and a neighbor woman from the next room remarked contemptuously, "He is no good."

No. 2. These are Poles. The woman makes knee pants of grammar-schoolboy size; she receives sixteen cents a dozen pairs. Two dozen are as many as she ever gets done in a day.

No. 3. They are Italians here, and are at work on knee pants. This woman receives sixteen cents a dozen pairs for most of them, but for some extra nice ones she gets eighteen cents a dozen. She has two dozen brought to her from the sweater's shop every day about two o'clock. She works from two in the afternoon until ten at night, and from six in the morning until noon the next day, to complete her allowance, for which she receives from thirty-two to thirty-six cents. The rent is a dollar and seventy-five cents per week; she has two children.

No. 4. This woman makes men's pants at twelve cents a pair. Formerly, when she was stronger, she could drive herself through six pairs a day; but now, with a little babe to look after, she can get only four pairs done. The room is intolerably dirty; but how can you have the heart to blame her?

No. 5. Polish Jews. The woman makes knee pants, working from seven in the morning till ten o'clock at night, and nets from twenty-seven to forty-four cents a day.

No. 6. Italians. This woman is an expert

seamstress. She is finishing men's coats at six cents apiece; and with nothing to bother her, working sixteen hours a day, she makes fifty-four cents. The rent for the narrow little back room is one dollar and thirty-five cents per week.

If you want variety, we will climb four flights of stairs, with half the plastering knocked off the walls, and talk with an English woman. She is working on fine cloth pants; she gets thirteen cents a pair; by working till very late in the evening, she can complete four pairs a day, and thinks it would be almost a paradise if she could make her fifty-two cents every day; but it is one of the characteristics of a sweater to systematically keep all his people hungry for work, and she seldom is able to get more than twelve pairs a week. She lives alone in a little sweat-box under the roof, for which she pays a dollar and a quarter per week.

Not far away, up two flights, we find a Portuguese widow, with four little girls, the eldest fifteen, the next thirteen, and the younger ones three and six, respectively; they are all dwarfed by hardship and insufficient food, so that the one who is fifteen is not larger than an average girl of twelve. The mother is sick, and the girls are trying to keep the wolf from the door by carrying on the sewing. They are all hard at work; they carry the pants back and forth themselves, and so for the most of their work receive twelve cents, though for some they get only ten cents a pair. They have only two little rooms with the most meagre furniture; the rent is one dollar and a half per week, and the sick mother and four girls huddle together in the one bed at night. They are pretty, bright-faced, intelligent girls, and with a fair chance would grow into strong, noble women; but one shudders when he takes into consideration the fearful odds against which they will have to struggle in this poverty-stricken, crime-cursed alley.

Here is another case of a similar description only a few blocks away. We go up three narrow flights, steep and dark, for space is as important in a low-class Boston tenement house as in a sardine box. The stairway is slippery from filth on the last flight, for on a small bench at the top, in a dry-goods box, a little

boy is raising squabs for the market, and the pigeon business, however much it may help

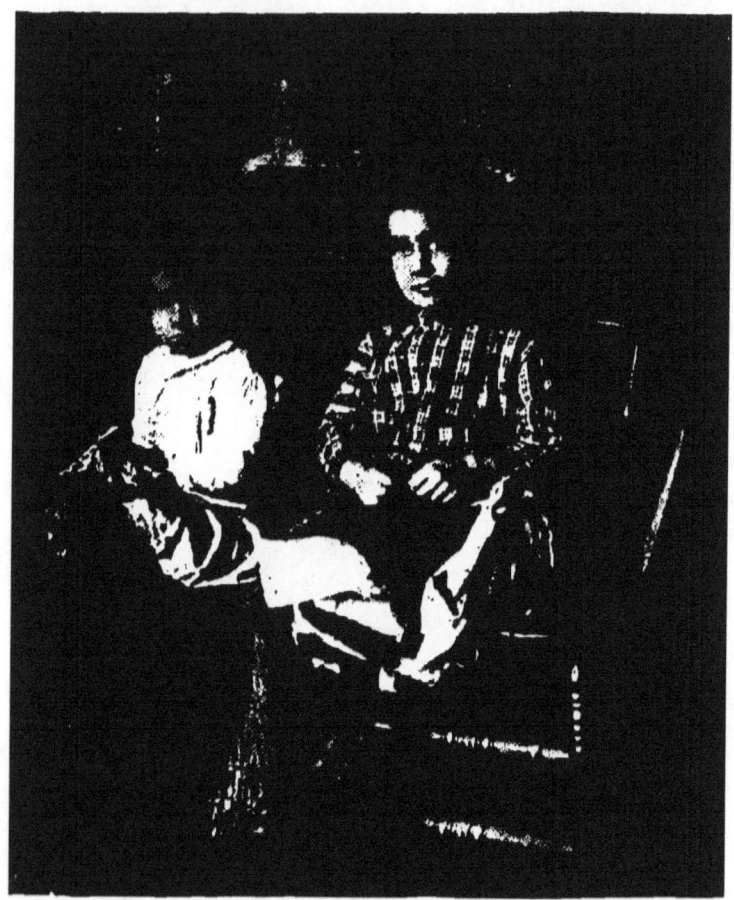

LITTLE CHILDREN FINISHING PANTS.

to pay the rent, is not conducive to cleanliness. We find here a suite of three little rooms, the largest of which is not more than 10 × 10; the others are much smaller. In these three little pigeon boxes eight people live, at least sleep — five men and boys, and a mother and two girls. The men are off most of the day, and work at such jobs as they find; the mother and little girls make pants for another leading Boston clothing house. The two little girls, the younger only three years, are both overcasting seams. The three make on an average sixteen pairs of pants a week, for which they get thirteen cents a pair; the young pigeon fancier, already spoken of, carrying the goods to and fro. The rent of these crowded quarters is two dollars and a quarter per week. In the same building, down-stairs, we went into a room which could not have been more than 10 × 12, where an American woman, with seven young women helping her, was at work dressmaking. We could not discover whether they were working for the stores or not, but the air was poisonous, and the workers had that deadly pallor which comes from habitually breathing bad air and from lack of sufficient food.

Sickness, to be dreaded anywhere, is espe-

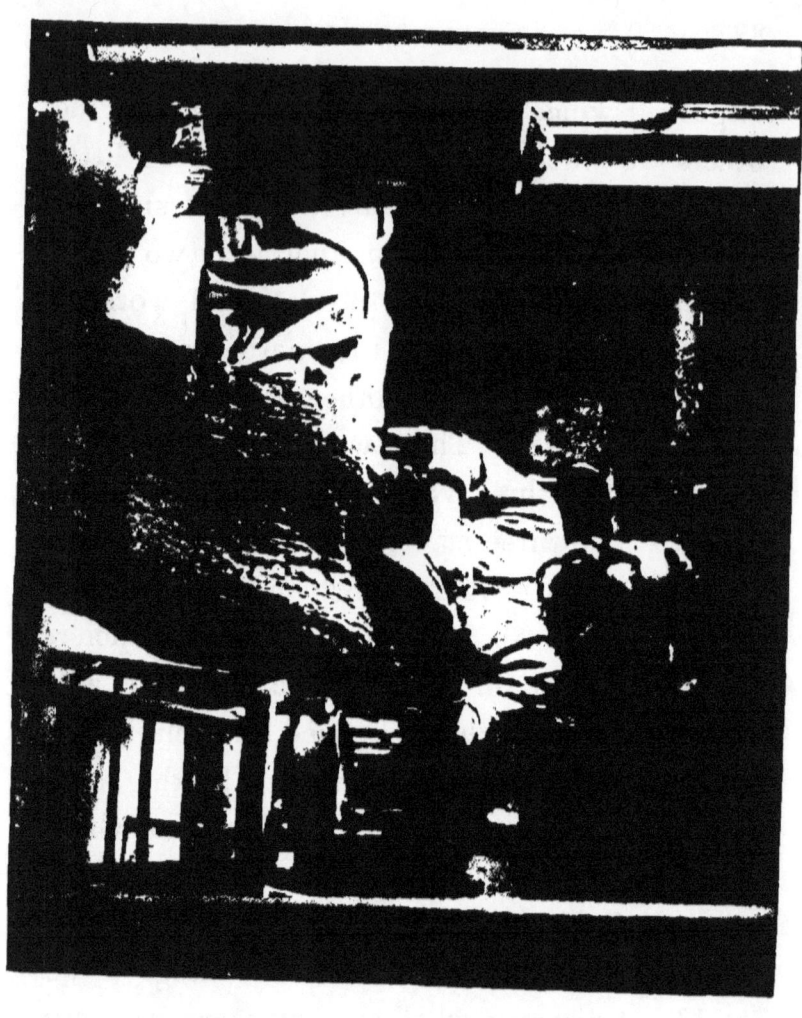

cially pitiful among these sweaters' slaves in the city. In the country the fresh air, fragrant with the breath of new-mown hay, or sweetened from ten thousand clover blossoms, is free to the poorest, but to be sick in a tenement house is something terrible. Yet crowded quarters, poisonous air, and filthy clothing make sickness a common guest in such places. I climbed one day up two flights into a dirty little room, the smell of which was sickening to me in three minutes, and yet there I found a man on a little cot (that had been given by the charitable missionary who guided me) who has been lying there for more than three years. For two years and more he had not even a cot, but lay on the floor in his dirt and pain. There are two children, too young to be of much assistance; the wife and mother sews, finishing pants for a rich Washington Street firm. She gets twelve, and sometimes, on fine, custom-made pants, thirteen cents a pair. She has worked so hard and continuously on poor food and with insufficient clothing, that rheumatism has settled in the joints of her fingers and stiffened them, till she is only able to turn off nine or ten pairs a week. Last week she could only make a dollar and fifteen cents; the rent was a dollar and a quarter. They have absolutely none of the ordinary comforts of life; the sick man has no sheets for his cot, and the rheumatic mother sleeps with her children on the floor.

Down-stairs, we look in on a mother and two grown daughters who are finishing pants for another fashionable firm, one which does a large business with clergymen. They are paid thirteen cents a pair, ordinarily, and for the very finest custom-made pants they receive as high as twenty cents, but complain, as it takes so much longer with the fine pants, that from two to three pairs is as much as one woman can complete in a day. There is a helpless air about this mother and her daughters that is very depressing.

There has been quite a controversy recently as to where the new United States postal uniforms for the Boston carriers were made. I settled this question to my own satisfaction during the past week, when, in company with Dr. Luther T. Townsend, of Boston University, and two other gentlemen, one of them being an Italian interpreter, I climbed the rickety stairs of an old North End tenement house, and found the pants for these same uni-

POSTAL UNIFORMS.

forms being made by Italian women at *nine and a half cents a pair!* They received them from a Jewish sweater. One of these women says that, by beginning at four o'clock in the morning and frequently working until twelve o'clock at night, she can make six pairs of these pants in a day. She has five children; the rent is two dollars per week. The husband has been out of work for eight months; the only one of the children who is able to earn anything is a boy who is a bootblack, and can earn, in fine weather, three dollars a week. Another woman at work on these postal uniforms, who was not able to labor quite such long hours, could only make four pairs a day. She also had five children, the only one able to earn anything being a daughter, fourteen years of age, who works in a sweater's shop for two dollars a week.

On the walls of the rooms in this building where the postal uniforms were being made, the cockroaches were crawling, and in some places were swarming as thick as ants about an anthill.

I have my note-books full of many other cases, including Portuguese, Italian, English, Polish, and a few Irish and American women, of the same general character as those already related; but a similar wicked scale of prices runs through the making of other clothing. I called on a woman in South Boston last week who was making overalls for a city firm at sixty cents a dozen pairs. They are the large variety of overalls, such as expressmen and such workers use, with straps going over the shoulders. I took a tape-line and carefully measured the sewing on one pair of these overalls. When they come to the seamstress, there has not been a stitch taken in them — they are simply cut out. There are thirty separate and distinct seams to be sewed, making in the aggregate thirty-two and a half feet of sewing, for which she receives the gross amount of five cents, out of which she has to pay the carrying to and fro. If she goes after them herself, she can bring only two dozen at a time, which will cost her ten cents car-fare, going and coming. When sent by express in a package of five or six dozen — the number she is able to make in a week — she is charged fifteen cents expressage each way, so that the expressage eats up the making of six pairs. In addition to this, the stiff cloth is very hard on machine needles, and she will break about ten cents worth per week. This woman's story is a sad one. Her husband, who was a strong, hard-working man, fell ill through an over-strain, and died after fifteen months' sickness, two months ago. She has three little children, the oldest four years and the youngest a little over a year. Work as hard as she can, driving her machine until late into the night, she is able to make only five dozen pairs of overalls a week, which, when expressage and breakage of needles are taken out, leaves her two dollars and sixty-five cents. The rent is a dollar and a half, which leaves one dollar and fifteen cents for the food and clothing of a mother and three children. Of course she cannot live on that, and would starve to death if she were not assisted by charity. And yet there is a firm doing business in South Boston mean enough to take advantage of the fact that people living in this part of the city are compelled to pay carfare or expressage on work secured in the city proper, and so has reduced the price for work given out in South Boston to *fifty cents a dozen pairs.*

I talked with another young woman, who has made overalls for both these firms, and has been compelled to give it up through sickness brought on from the confinement and strained position of sitting so many hours a day over a sewing-machine. This poor girl told me that both of these firms were now giving a great part of this class of work to the public authorities in charge of the House of Correction, to be done by the prisoners, and that a daily stint for a woman in prison is only eight pairs. This sick, discouraged girl, in a most heart-breaking way, said she thought she would better commit some crime in order to procure a place in the House of Correction, for there she would have much better quarters, a great deal nicer food, and would only have to make eight pairs a day, while at home she must force herself to make at least a dozen pairs a day, or starve.

Fellow-citizens, what do you think of this? Is there not something wrong in a system of things that permits the authorities of the State or city to enter into competition with the sewing-women of Boston at such a cruel and heartless rate that no woman can work at it and keep out of prison, unless she is assisted by charity? This same South Boston firm gives out men's shirts to be made at sixty cents a dozen. The material for one of these shirts costs twenty-three cents, the making five cents — a total of twenty-eight cents. They retail these shirts at fifty cents apiece, making a net profit of twenty-two cents on an investment of twenty-eight cents for a few weeks' time.

During the last few weeks, as I have gone about among these women, my ears have been haunted with that old song of Thomas Hood, as appropriate now, in the latter part of the nineteenth century, in the city of Boston, as it ever has been anywhere, at any time, in the history of human greed.

>   With fingers weary and worn,
>   With eyelids heavy and red,
>   A woman sat, in unwomanly rags,
>   Plying her needle and thread —
>   Stitch! stitch! stitch!
>   In poverty, hunger, and dirt;
>   And still with a voice of dolorous pitch
>   She sang the "Song of the Shirt!"
>
>   "Work! work! work!
>   While the cock is crowing aloof!
>   And work — work — work,
>   Till the stars shine through the roof!
>   It's, oh! to be a slave
>   Along with the barbarous Turk,
>   Where woman has never a soul to save,
>   If this is Christian work!

"Work — work — work!
  Till the brain begins to swim!
Work — work — work
  Till the eyes are heavy and dim!

  Stitch — stitch — stitch,
  In poverty, hunger, and dirt, —
  Sewing at once, with a double thread,
  A shroud as well as a shirt!

"But why do I talk of death,
  That phantom of grisly bone?
  I hardly fear his terrible shape,
  It seems so like my own —
  It seems so like my own
  Because of the fast I keep:
  O God! that bread should be so dear,
  And flesh and blood so cheap!

"Work — work — work!
  My labor never flags;
  And what are its wages? A bed of straw,
  A crust of bread — and rags,
  That shattered roof — and this naked floor —
  A table — a broken chair —
  And a wall so blank my shadow I thank
  For sometimes falling there!

"Work — work — work
  From weary chime to chime!
Work — work — work
  As prisoners work for crime!"

If Thomas Hood had lived in our day, and could have gone around with me in Boston, he would have had to make it stronger yet, for among us the good, honest sewing-woman must work at least one-third harder than the "prisoners work for crime." And on such wages the prayer with which he continues must be forever unanswered: —

> "Oh! but to breathe the breath
> Of the cowslip and primrose sweet —
> With the sky above my head,
> And the grass beneath my feet!
> For only one short hour
> To feel as I used to feel,
> Before I knew the woes of want,
> And the walk that costs a meal!

> "Oh! but for one short hour, —
> A respite, however brief!
> No blessed leisure for love or hope,
> But only time for grief!
> A little weeping would ease my heart;
> But in their briny bed
> My tears must stop, for every drop
> Hinders needle and thread!"

> With fingers weary and worn,
> With eyelids heavy and red,
> A woman sat, in unwomanly rags,
> Plying her needle and thread —
> Stitch! stitch! stitch!
> In poverty, hunger, and dirt;
> And still with a voice of dolorous pitch,—
> Would that its voice could reach the rich! —
> She sang this "Song of the Shirt."

II

LETTER OF CRITICISM

"Slavery ain't o' nary color,
  'Tain't the hide that makes it wus,
 All it keers fer in a feller
  'S jest to make him fill its pus."

   JAMES RUSSELL LOWELL : *Biglow Papers.*

II
LETTER OF CRITICISM

BOSTON, June 29, 1891.

REV. LOUIS ALBERT BANKS, *St. John's M. E. Church, South Boston, Mass.*

Dear Sir: — In the sermon which you preached yesterday, the title, as given in the newspapers, is "The *White Slaves of Boston* Sweaters." Under the fourteenth amendment to the Constitution of the United States there can be no such thing as "*slave*" in this country. Under the decision of Judge Parsons there has not been a slave in Massachusetts since the adoption of the Constitution. I therefore venture to ask you some questions.

1. How do you justify the term "*white slave*" when applied to the persons whose condition you describe?

2. "Climb three flights to an attic suite of two rooms, and there one would find a mother and five children" doubtless in very bad condi-

tion; the mother trying to support them; the tenement doubtless very bad. Suppose we condemn the tenement, — pull it down, — then these people would have *no* roof over their heads. Is *no* roof better than *some kind* of a roof? Suppose we refuse to trust her to make pants? Is *no* work better than *some* work?

3. The mother earns her living, or part of it, by making "pants." Pants made in this way are sold at a very low price at retail, after being subjected to the cost of distribution in the customary way. There is great competition in this business. That competition leads every employer to pay the highest wages that can be recovered from the sale of the pants, also allowing the sweater's charge. If the cost of making is advanced on this class of pants, they cannot be sold at all; then there would be no sweater, and the woman would get no work. Is *no* work better than *some* work?

4. The sweater deals as a middleman with the manufacturer and the worker. If he did not deal with this kind of work, it would cost the manufacturer more to reach the worker than it does now; no sweater would be em-

ployed if he did not earn what he makes; then the manufacturer, or clothier, could pay *less* for making the pants, because he now pays *all that the trade will bear.* If it cost him more to reach the worker, he *must* pay less. Suppose we abolish the sweater, or middleman, then he would not distribute the work, and there would be *no* work. Is that better than *some* work?

5. Suppose this woman had not come here with her children and had stayed, perhaps, in Italy or in Russia, instead of coming here. Is *some* work *here* better than *no* work in *Italy?*

6. If the mother cannot support the children, — being now in this country without having been sent back, — she is entitled to go with her children to the almshouse, where suitable shelter, clean rooms, and good food would be provided. Is it better for her to *try to support her children* under existing conditions *than to go to the almshouse?*

7. There is an ample supply of money available for purposes of true charity. Does not true charity consist in refusing to give alms to those who can or may support themselves? Is it better to give alms to those people in their attic,

or to give alms to them under the conditions of the almshouse? Which course would be most sure to pauperize them utterly?

8. The use of the term "slave" implies a slave-owner and a slave-driver. In this series of (1) *the manufacturer*, (2) *the sweater* or *middleman*, and (3) *the working-woman with her children*, which is the slave-owner and which is the slave-driver? Under what authority does the slave-master force this woman to render her labor for all that it is worth?

9. If her work is worth more than she gets, can she not get it?

A little inquiry into the condition of the clothing trade, and some examination of the fact, might disclose to you that the poor sewing-woman is poor because she sews poorly, and that there is always a scarcity of skilful and intelligent sewing-women, at full wages.

My final question is, how do you propose to help those who are incapable of helping themselves, without pauperizing them yet more than they are pauperized under their present conditions? What will you do when you have destroyed the house and done away with the sweater? .

Are you justified, as a Christian minister, in creating a prejudice and arousing malignant passion by the use of the term "*slave?*" Can you defend or justify this term, under the conditions that are reported, as they are stated in the printed report of your sermon?

I venture to put these questions to you because I think that the dangerous class in this community is to be found among persons who, without intelligence, create animosity, and by their method of preaching tend to retard rather than to promote the progress of the poor and ignorant in this country.

Very sincerely yours,

* * * * *

III

REPLY TO A CRITICISM ON "THE WHITE SLAVES OF BOSTON SWEATERS"

"Freedom's secret wilt thou know? —
Counsel not with flesh and blood;
Loiter not for cloak or food;
Right thou feelest, rush to do."

RALPH WALDO EMERSON: *Freedom.*

III

REPLY TO A CRITICISM ON "THE WHITE SLAVES OF THE BOSTON SWEATERS"

AMONG the scores of thankful letters which I have received, commenting on the discourse on "The White Slaves of the Boston Sweaters," there is one of an entirely different character, written by a distinguished writer on social questions, a gentleman for whom I have always entertained the highest respect. I should be very glad to give the name of the author of this letter; but as it is marked "personal," I cannot, in honor, do so.

This letter so clearly and unswervingly outlines and defends the extreme conservative side of this question, that I feel I cannot do a better service to the cause of the "sweater's victim" than to answer it in this public way. My critic begins by assailing the title of the discourse. He says: "In the sermon which you preached yesterday, the title as given in the newspapers is 'The White Slaves of the Boston Sweaters.' Under the fourteenth amendment to the Constitution of the United States, there can be no such thing as 'slave' in this country. Under the decision of Judge Parsons there has not been a slave in Massachusetts since the adoption of the Constitution." Wonderful Judge Parsons! who is able, by the magic wand of his decision, to unshackle all the slaves who, under the cruel whip of necessity, — more unmerciful than any slave-driver's lash, — have sweated under the burdens imposed by avaricious task-masters in every city of the commonwealth.

Can you make men free by constitution simply? Are there no slaves except those who, like the African thirty years ago, are bought and sold at the auction block? Ay, indeed! for every black man liberated by President Lincoln's proclamation, there is, to-day, a white man robbed and degraded and brutalized by some gigantic trust or other equally soulless, unfeeling, corporate power.

For every mother whose heart was broken by

having her children wrenched from her arms in the African slave-market, there is a white mother, whose very soul is crushed at the sight of her hungry, ragged, little ones. For every black babe torn from its mother's breast by the iniquitous system of negro slavery, the slums of our great cities have a white child, whose future is equally dark and hopeless.

My critic's first question is, "How do you justify the term 'white slave' when applied to the persons whose condition you describe?" My answer is very simple. If a widow with little children to care for, who cannot go out to do other kinds of work, and is compelled to work eighteen hours a day for fifty cents, and dares not give this up for fear of starvation to her children, is not a slave, then will somebody tell me what element is lacking to make slavery?

The second question is as follows: "'Climb three flights to an attic suite of two rooms, and there one would find a mother and five children,' doubtless in very bad condition; the mother trying to support them; the tenement doubtless very bad. Suppose we condemn the tenement, — pull it down, — then these people will have no roof over their heads. Is *no* roof

A TENEMENT-HOUSE COURT.

better than *some kind* of a roof? Suppose we refuse to trust her to make pants — is *no* work better than *some* work?"

To the first part of this question, relating to the roof of this bad tenement house, I answer frankly: Yes, no roof is better. This poor woman, working at starvation-wages, is furnishing from twelve to twenty per cent interest on the money invested in this miserable old rookery, whose heartless landlord, like the unjust judge of the Gospels, fears not God and regards not man. If we condemn this disease-breeding death-trap, it will not be a question of this woman having "no roof" over her head, but she may have a decent roof, with healthful, sanitary regulations, at a less rent than she now pays, and still pay an honest interest on the investment to the landlord. As to the second part of the question, "Is no work better than some work?" that is not a fair putting of the question. Our modern Christian civilization does not dare to put it that way. It is not a question of no work, or some work. We must furnish this woman some work, at such just and rightful wages as shall give her and her children bread to eat and raiment to put on, and a decent, though it be humble, roof over their heads.

We pass to our critic's third question: "The mother earns her living, or a part of it, by making 'pants.' Pants made in this way are sold at a very low price at retail, after being subjected to the cost of distribution in the customary way. There is great competition in this business. That competition leads every employer to pay the highest wages that can be recovered from the sale of the pants, also allowing the sweater's charge. If the cost of making is advanced on this class of pants, they cannot be sold at all; then there would be no sweater, and the woman would get no work. Is *no* work better than *some* work?" The trouble with a great deal of this is, that it is incorrect both in its premise and in its reasoning. It is indeed true that there is great competition in the clothing business, but it is not true that the result of this competition leads every employer to pay the highest wages that can be recovered from the sale of the pants. It is also a remarkable statement to make, that if the cost is advanced, then there will be no more pants made. Can my critic really believe that the whole of mankind would suddenly go "pantless" if the price for making them were raised to a point where the sewing-woman could make a decent living? It is also a curious statement to make that "If there were no sweater, the woman would get no work." The sweater is a comparatively recent institution, and I devoutly believe an institution of the devil. Before the sweater came to be a factor in the situation, the woman had work, and better pay than she now receives. The incoming of the sweater has not resulted in more work, but in less wages.

If my critic will take the trouble to examine the testimony given before the committee appointed by the English House of Lords, which may be found in the Public Library, he will see that it is the universal testimony of hundreds of witnesses that the sweater is an unnecessary factor in the manufacturing trades, and that in every department of the labor world where the sweating system has been introduced, the wages of the laborer have been reduced from forty to seventy per cent.

The fourth question is similar to the third: "The sweater deals as a middleman with the manufacturer and the worker. If he did not deal with this kind of work, it would cost the manufacturer more to reach the worker than it does now. No sweater would be employed if he did not earn what he makes. Then the manufacturer, or clothier, could pay less for making the pants, because he now pays all the trade will bear. If it cost him more to reach the worker, he must pay less. Suppose we abolish the sweater, or middleman, then he would not distribute the work, and there would be *no* work. Is that better than *some* work?"

I have already answered this question in part. It is not correct that it would cost the manufacturer more to reach the worker without the sweater than with him. It is also ridiculous to suppose that if the sweater were abolished there would be no work. The demand for clothing would be just the same without the sweater as with him. Besides that, everything that takes the employer away from the people who do his work, and removes him from contact with them, is a bad thing, and always bodes ill to any harmonious relation between capital and labor. I am satisfied that there are proprietors in Boston firms, who, if they could go around with me, and see, as I have seen, the poverty and suffering of the sweaters' slaves who are making up their goods, would revolt against the whole system. It is only the sweater who comes in contact with these people, and the sweater is, as a rule, greedy and avaricious, and hardened against all humane feeling.

We pass to the fifth question: "Suppose this woman had not come here with her children, and had stayed, perhaps, in Italy or in Russia, instead of coming here. Is *some* work *here* better than *no* work in *Italy?*" Very likely it is true that the woman is as well off here as she would be in Italy. But is *Italy* to be the standard of our American civilization? I stood on a bridge over the Tiber, fronting the famous castle of St. Angelo in Rome, on a hot Sunday morning in July, and watched a company of people on a barge who were driving piles in the river. There were about eighty men and women, the sexes about equally divided, pulling and tugging away, in the hot sun, at ropes and pulleys, in order to lift the heavy iron hammer and drop it on the head of the piling. In Boston there would have been a little donkey engine, and one or two men to look after it all the crew that would have

SUNDAY ON NORTH STREET.

been needed. Shall we go back to Italy for a model? Furthermore, this Italian woman is setting up a standard of life for all laboring women. It is not enough to say she is as well off here as in Italy. We cannot afford to permit the establishing of little Italian centres throughout the Republic, with which every American laborer in the land must enter into competition. No matter where people came from, nor what they have suffered in their native land, if we permit them to come to us, we are compelled, in sheer self-defence, to see that they are treated fairly and justly, and receive a sufficient compensation for their toil to support them in cleanliness, intelligence, and morality.

Question six raises a different problem: "If the mother cannot support the children, — being now in this country, without having been sent back, — she is entitled to go with her children to the almshouse, where suitable shelter, clean rooms, and good food will be provided. Is it better for her to *try to support her children*, under existing conditions, than to go to the almshouse?" It is, of course, better for the woman to try to support her children. The almshouse is for the sick and helplessly infirm. Such may go there in all honor, without disgrace. I doubt not there are men in the almshouse who have done more service to humanity than many others who die amid luxury and wealth.

But nothing can be more vicious than to speak of people who are able and willing to work as candidates for the almshouse, because the cruel oppression in their wages makes it impossible for them to support themselves. It is not charity these people need or want; it is justice. True, Christ said, "The poor ye have always with you," and it is probable that we shall always need to support by charity the crippled, the insane, and the unfortunate, but it is a certain indication of rottenness in any civilization that makes charity necessary for a man or woman who is able and willing to work.

The seventh question continues this same thought with variations: "There is an ample supply of money available for purposes of true charity. Does not true charity consist in refusing to give alms to those who can, or may, support themselves? Is it better to give alms to these people, in their attic, or to give alms to them under the conditions of the almshouse? What course would be most sure to pauperize them utterly?" For once, my critic and myself are in agreement. I believe it is better for one to partly support himself than not to do anything towards it. Nothing is more demoralizing to any one than to become accustomed to receive charity. But, after all, you may pauperize people almost as rapidly in the attic as in the almshouse. It is against the whole system that I make war. I do not admit, for a moment, that it is necessary for the sewing-woman to receive such wages as to compel her starvation, unless alms be given to her in her attic.

In the discourse which is thus criticised I showed plainly that the aprons for which the seamstress received, net, one cent for making, returned a profit of fifteen cents, on an investment of ten cents by her employer. Now, I do not admit that the rigors of competition are so great that it compels this manufacturer to make one hundred and fifty per cent profit while this woman toils sixteen hours a day to make forty-five cents.

I showed that the women who make shirts made only fifty cents a day, and yet the proprietor made on every shirt twenty-two cents profit on an investment of twenty-eight cents. I do not admit that competition is so stern that it is necessary for this shirt manufacturer to make seventy-eight per cent profit while the woman who works for him must beg assistance of the Provident Association, or see her children cry for bread.

Or, take the case of the poor girl, whose mother finishes pants for the postal uniforms at nine and one-half cents a pair, slaving eighteen hours for fifty-seven cents; and she, the daughter, toils all day long, in the midst of the physical and moral stench of a Jewish sweater's shop, for sixteen and two-thirds cents. But she is better off than the orphan girl that works beside her, whose condition some poet has described : —

> " Left there, nobody's daughter,
>   Child of disgrace and shame,
> Nobody ever taught her
>   A mother's sweet saving name.
>
> Nobody ever caring
>   Whether she stood or fell,
> And men (are they men ?) ensnaring
>   With the arts and the gold of hell!
>
> Stitching with ceaseless labor
>   To earn her pitiful bread;
> Begging a crust of a neighbor,
>   And getting a curse instead!

All through the long, hot summer,
   All through the cold, dark time,
With fingers that numb and number
   Grow, white as the frost's white rime.

Nobody ever conceiving
   The throb of that warm, young life,
Nobody ever believing
   The strain of that terrible strife!

Nobody kind words pouring
   In that orphan heart's sad ear;
But all of us all ignoring
   What lies at our door so near!"

There is nothing wholesome in the question whether it is better to pauperize people a little in the attic, or to pauperize them altogether in the almshouse. We ought not to pauperize them at all. A noble Christian woman, who has a young men's Bible class in the North End, and who by her womanly tact and Christian sympathy has gained the confidence of some of the most hopeless cases in that section, told me that one of these boys said to her, "When the Back Bay folks know that we are made of flesh and blood, they won't pauperize us any longer."

The eighth question returns in some of its aspects to the first: "The use of the term 'slave' implies a slave-owner and a slave-driver. In this series of the manufacturer, the sweater or middleman, and the working-woman with her children, which is the slave-owner, and which is the slave-driver? Under

CLARK'S MISSION.

what authority does the slave-master force this woman to render her labor for all that it is worth?" Answering the last part of the question first, I have already shown that the woman does not get all that her work is worth. The manufacturer, who makes from seventy-eight to a hundred and fifty per cent profit, gets a far larger proportion of the profits than rightly belongs to him.

Under the sweating system, the sweater is, most emphatically, both the slave-master and slave-driver; and no Georgia overseer was ever more cruel than some of these sweater taskmasters in Boston to-day.

Even at the wretched wages they pay, they will not give any of their workers all the work they can do; they dole out the work to them, trying to make them think it is very scarce. If they ask for higher pay, they are met at once with a threat of discharge. Do you ask why they do not hunt for something better? What can a poor, half-broken-down mother, with three little babies, do hunting work? Who will pay the rent, furnish them food, and care for the children while she makes her search? There are thousands of laboring people, both men and women, in all our great cities, who are in the same condition that a majority of the Israelites were when Moses came to them, and told the marvellous story of his talk with Jehovah, and painted before their dim eyes the picture of the Canaan, and recounted to their dull ears the promise of their deliverance from bondage. Pathetic, indeed, is the record, "They hearkened not unto Moses for anguish of spirit and for cruel bondage." It is idle to talk, as so many newspapers as well as private individuals do, as though domestic service were the cure-all for these half-starving, underpaid women. A great majority of the women who are slaves to these sweaters, have families of little children depending on them, that are as dear to their hearts as are the children of more fortunate mothers to them. Dr. Barnardo, of London, who has had a most extensive experience among the poor, tells of a poor woman, with a husband lying disabled in the hospital, earning her living by charing and odd jobs, while she herself was receiving out-door hospital relief for physical debility. Driven at last to accept assistance from the relieving officer, she hastened home, placed the bread and meat on a table, and fell dead of exhaustion. Dr. Barnardo was sent for, and beside the dead body of the mother he was surprised, as well he might be, to find five well-fed, chubby children. The poor, slum mother had literally starved herself to death that her children might live! Truly, as Coleridge says, "A mother is the holiest thing alive;" and God never intended that the almshouse or the orphan asylum should be the only refuge held open for a mother who is able and willing to work to support her children.

In the ninth question our critic says: "If her work is worth more than she gets, can she not get it? A little inquiry into the condition of the clothing trade and some examination of the facts might disclose to you that the poor sewing-woman is poor because she sews poorly, and that there is always a scarcity of skilful and intelligent sewing-women, at full wages." The more thorough my examination into the facts of the case, the more I am convinced that the sweating system is demoralizing the entire clothing trade, as it will every trade it touches. Whether the woman sews poorly or not, she does not, in any class she may be placed, receive the wages to which she is entitled.

The conclusion of my critic's letter is, I think, as remarkable as anything in it. He says: "My final question is, how do you propose to help those who are incapable of helping themselves, without pauperizing them yet more than they are pauperized under their present conditions? What will you do when you have

NORTH END JUNK SHOP.

destroyed the house and done away with the sweater?" To this part of the concluding question I simply say, I will be a Christian, and pay honest wages for honest work. But the critic continues: "Are you justified, as a

Christian minister, in creating prejudice and arousing malignant passion by the use of the term 'slave?' Can you defend or justify this term under the conditions as they are stated in the printed report of your sermon? I venture to put these questions to you because I think that the dangerous class in this community is to be found among persons who, without intelligence, create animosity and, by their method of preaching, tend to retard rather than to promote the progress of the poor and ignorant in this country."

My answer to all that is, that, as a Christian minister, I am a follower of Him, who, standing in the midst of the self-satisfied and wealthy oppressors of His times, exclaimed, "Woe unto you, Pharisees! for ye tithe mint and rue and all manner of herbs, and pass over judgment and the love of God." And who, standing in the audience of all the people, said unto His disciples, "Beware of the Scribes which devour widows' houses, and for a show make long prayers: the same shall receive greater damnation;" who, standing in the presence of the lawyers, cried aloud, "Woe unto you, also, ye lawyers! for ye lade men with burdens grievous to be borne, and ye yourselves touch not the burdens with one of your fingers." I am a follower of Him who came "not to send peace on the earth, but a sword." All an infernal system of oppression, like the sweating system, asks, is to be let alone. To uncover its atrocities is like turning over a huge stone in the meadow in springtime, that has been a hiding-place for bugs and worms that nest away in the dark. As soon as the hot, searching sunlight finds them, they will wriggle and squirm in agony until they can crawl under cover again. So I do not wonder that, when the hideous cruelty of the tenement-house sweat-shop is brought to light, the sweater and all his friends wriggle and squirm in an agony of fright and shame. Neither am I alarmed that this critic, as a type of conservatism, regards me as a member of the most dangerous class in the community. It was ever thus. The old anti-slavery agitators were considered the most dangerous men in the republic, and I remember that a very distinguished minister once bitterly regretted the agitation on the evils of slavery, because he feared it would destroy the prospect

HOME OF THE MATHERS.

for a revival of religion in the city where he lived.

If to be a Christian minister is to stand as a

policeman to hold back the righteous indignation of the robbed and degraded laborer, o[r]
preach patience and contentment to empt[y]
stomachs, — empty that the sweater may gro[w]
rich and fat on the toil of orphans and widow[s]
— then I spurn the title as beneath the dignit[y]
of my manhood; but if, as I take it, to be [a]
Christian minister is to be like my Master, th[e]
brother of all men, rich or poor, standing fo[r]
ever as the unflinching enemy of oppressio[n]
and injustice wherever found, as the friend an[d]
advocate of the defenceless and the weak, the[n]
I am proud of the title, and thank God for it[s]
unspeakable privilege.

IV

THE PLAGUE OF THE SWEAT-SHOP

"Can the heart be deformed, and contract incurable ugliness and infirmity under the pressure of disproportionate misfortune, like the spine beneath too low a vault?" — VICTOR HUGO: *Les Misérables.*

IV

THE PLAGUE OF THE SWEAT-SHOP

THE Klamath Lake Indians in Oregon have a strange and weird fashion of mourning their dead. They dig a hole in the ground, and roof it over with willows, which they cover with dirt, forming a sort of underground cabin. In case of death in the family, the relatives go into this dug-out, which is called a "sweat-lodge," and heated rocks are brought in and heaped in the centre of the lodge, and water sprinkled over them, so as to fill the room with steam. In the midst of this steam-heated, poisonous air the family hover around their heap of rocks, and sweat for days at a time, in memory of their departed friends.

When the mourning days are over, they heap up into a cairn beside the sweat-lodge the stones that have been used, as a monument to their dead.

But that, after all, is only a brief torture which is soon over, and is constantly lightened by the hope of relief. The sweat-lodge of our modern civilization is a much more serious matter. The tortured victims who are suffering there, are not mourning for their dead friends, but for the living, and in the dark night of their sorrow there is no promise of a brighter dawn.

The word "sweater" derives its origin from the Anglo-Saxon word *swat,* and means the separation or extraction of labor or toil from others, for one's own benefit. Any person who employs others to extract from them surplus labor without compensation, is a sweater. A middleman-sweater is a person who acts as a contractor of such labor for another man. The position becomes aggravated when the middleman-sweater, as is usually the case in the modern sweat-shop, employs the labor himself, at his own house, for the purpose of extracting a double quantity of labor, either by lowering wages or working longer hours.

An English writer gives this definition of the sweating system: "One whereby the middleman tries to get the largest profit, with the least labor and outlay, out of the maximum labor of his workers." Another gives three definitions: " First, one who grinds the face of the poor; second, a man who contributes neither capital, skill, nor speculation, and yet gets a profit; third, a middleman." Still another describes it as a systematized payment of unfair wages. Away back in the days of Queen Anne the term "sweater" was given to a certain class of street ruffian. The sweaters went about in small bands, and, forming a circle around an inoffensive wayfarer, pricked him with their swords, and compelled him to dance till he perspired from the exertion. The sweater is still a ruffian, though the street is no longer the scene of action, but, in some attic or tenement-house bedroom, he gathers his victims from the poorest and most helpless of our population.

It is my purpose, first of all this morning, to show you something of the growth and development of the sweat-shop in England. It is reasonable for us to suppose that, if left to itself, it will produce the same general results in this country that it has there. Fortunately we have an abundance of data upon which to form our conclusions.

There are in the Boston Public Library five ponderous volumes containing the evidence taken before a commission, appointed by the English House of Lords, to examine into the sweating system of Great Britain.

I think it is well for American laboring-men to know that this evidence puts beyond question the fact that the sweating business, while it may begin with the clothing trade, by no means ends there. "The plague of the sweat-shop" is not something of interest to the tailors and sewing-women only, but is of equal importance to workers of every class. Take the matchbox trade; before the sweating days, the people who worked at it received two and three-fourths pence a gross. Now the large contractors let and sub-let until it is only one and a half pence a gross, and a woman and a family of children have to work all the week to make four or five shillings.

The fur trade in Europe has been largely driven into Whitechapel sweaters' shops.

They call the sweater in this business a "chamber master," and in these foul chambers, in the midst of "bad smells, great heat, no ventilation, and fetid refuse," men and women swelter and

THE PEANUTTER.

die, the men getting ten shillings, and the women about five shillings a week.

The cabinet and upholstery trade is not exempt. Sub-contracting here, as in clothing, is the first step in sweating. The evidence shows that sweating began in this business as early as 1855, but has rapidly increased under pauper immigration from Italy and Russia since 1880. Much of the work is crowded into garrets and cellars, where there are no sanitary arrangements. So universally is this so, that the sweater in this business is called a "garret master." Wages have been brought down, from forty to fifty shillings a week, to from eighteen to twenty shillings.

The boot and shoe trade has had the same history. Large numbers of foreigners are employed in this work. The workers are kept in ignorance of the language and under surveillance, so as to be taken advantage of. They are not instructed in the more skilled work, and, to use the words of one of the witnesses, "are too crushed to resist." They are compelled to work from eighteen to twenty hours a day. Wages in these sweat-shops are from ten to fifteen shillings a week.

In Sheffield, the great cutlery manufacturing city, the same system is prevailing, and a woman whose business was awl-blade grinding, a strong woman of forty-five years of age, testified that she could only make six and a half shillings per week.

Military harness and accoutrements are also made by the sweaters. Many workmen earn only three pence an hour, and complain that they cannot live on it. The nail trade is in the same condition. A man and wife working together make thirteen shillings a week. Women's earnings average from three shillings and a half to six shillings per week.

Large numbers of women are only able to earn three shillings a week at this business. Boys and girls are paid, in a sweater's chain-shop, one-half penny per hour.

A witness from Glasgow testified in regard to the clothing shops of that city: "It is a rule among the sweaters to give the men some money, a shilling, every night, to keep them alive till the next day. Some of the men at the end of the week are actually in debt instead of having anything coming to them. When in debt, they do not, as a rule, come back, but go to another sweater. The men never actually get any wages, but are in debt from one year's end till another. All independence is taken out of the men; they are always in the sweater's power."

A witness from Leeds says: "Wages are driven to a starvation level, and workmen at piece-work compelled to excessive hours. If the employers find a good workman, who is earning good wages by piece-work, they try to reduce prices. Time work is healthier, but no one would believe how the men are driven in shops where time-work exists."

Another gentleman, testifying about his investigations in Glasgow, tells of a place he visited, where a sweater had between forty and fifty women employed in an old boiler shed, a disused part of an engineer's shop; the women had to get to it by three wooden ladders, and had to go through a joiner's shop in order to enter the workroom. There was no sanitary accommodation for these women anywhere. It is a common practice for sweaters to take on learners, that is to say, to employ young girls for a certain time to learn the machine part of the work; but they get no wages for say five or six weeks or so, or two months, and after that time, if competent, they receive two or three shillings per week. But the sweater's trick, as soon as the busy season is over, is to discharge all these girls and take on a new batch.

The practical slavery to which the laboring-people, by the sweating system, have been degraded, is illustrated on almost every page of the evidence. One witness testifies: "They do almost as they like with their victims. The people are afraid to give evidence against them. The sweater is a law unto himself. One woman I came across says she has not been paid for her work done some three years ago, on some trivial pretext which the sweater made. Another deducted a whole week's work from a woman's wages because she was ten minutes late, and so aggravated the people in the neighborhood that they smashed his windows, showing the state of things between the sweater and his people."

As one would naturally expect, moral degradation keeps pace with the outrage upon the rights of the laborer. It is claimed that the Jewesses, who have always had the most unblemished character of any women in the world, are being ruined in the sweat-shops of London, where they are herded together with all classes of men in a way which renders morality and decency next to impossible. One witness bears this terrible testimony: "The sweating system, in which you have young girls working with men of all nationalities, and of all degrees of intelligence, conduces to their being later on, and they are mostly, to my certain knowledge, prostitutes. Most of the young English girls whom we can see in the Strand and Oxford Street are, or have been, tailoresses, and the conditions conduce to that effect."

So great and wide-spread is this question of the increase of immorality in England, under the reign of the sweat-shop, that a barrister-at-law, Mr. Wm. Thompson, has written a novel entitled, "The Sweater's Victim," which has for its burden the ruin of girls through the "plague of the sweat-shop."

It is easy to say, "Oh, well, these horrible things you are telling us about belong to the Old World!" I would to God they did belong to the Old World alone, but the horrible truth is, that this vicious system is like a banyan-tree that has run its roots under the sea, and is coming up, and blossoming, and flourishing in all our great American cities. Listen to this description of the slaves of the sweat-shop in

New York, given by the *New York Herald:* "In the lower portion of the great east side of this city, are hundreds of tall, ill-appearing tenement houses, in which thousands of half-starved, sunken-eyed men and women are crowded into small, foul, over-heated rooms, working day and night for just enough to keep body and soul together. Scattered among the workers are dirty children, and sometimes cats and dogs. Everything in these places has to stand aside for work. It is work, work, work, day and night, year in and year out. In these over-crowded rooms the air is poisoned with the heat from the stoves, the steam from the cooking, and the fumes of oil and gas. Very few of the toilers can speak English. They are the most wretched-looking, miserably-paid class of workers in America. They are foreigners, and come chiefly from Russia and Poland. No sunshine enters into their lives. Their existence is one hard, deep, grinding toil. They have no hope of brighter days to come. As they have worked for years, so they expect to work in the future. But the sweater does not care. He has his contracts with the manufacturers. Every day great bundles of clothing are dumped into these dens, and then the slaves are driven at full speed

INSIDE A SWEAT-SHOP.

to make them up. Competition is keen, but the sweater makes money."

The Journeymen Tailors' National Union, in its fifth annual report, describes in detail one of these New York sweat-shops, similar to those which the recent commission, appointed by the Governor of Massachusetts, found to be the manufactories of enormous quantities of clothing for Boston firms: " On the first floor, which was occupied by two families, was a contractor, or 'sweater,' who made overcoats. In the front room, 8×16 ft., eight full-grown men were at work, some on sewing-machines, a man pressing, and others finishing. They were hollow-cheeked and cadaverous. Trousers and undershirts were their only apparel. In the rear room, 9×14, were six other men, almost identical in appearance with those in the front. All were working as if for dear life.

"This place was simply indescribable in its filthiness. The only household furniture discernible (for the contractor and his family lived in the rooms), were a bedstead and a child's crib in one of the two dark, so-called bedrooms. Bedding and overcoats were piled up together. The floors were four inches deep with dirt and cotton battings and scraps of linings. The ceilings and woodwork looked as though they had not seen a brush since the house was built years ago. Water from the floor above had leaked through the ceiling, but it seemed to make no difference. One stove was used by the pressers and the cook. It did not appear that there was any regular meal hour. There was a table littered with dirty dishes, morsels of food, and scraps of coats. One man was seated, eating out of a dish with his fingers, without the aid of spoon, knife, or fork. As soon as he had finished, he merely wiped his hands on some cotton batting, and proceeded with his work. The poor creatures were haggard and apparently stupid." What wonder?

Dr. George C. Stiebling, of New York, who accompanied the recent Boston investigating committee, says, in an affidavit made after a careful investigation, that the New York sweatshops "in which clothing is manufactured, and which serve at the same time as dwelling-rooms for the bosses, their families, and boarders, are overcrowded, ill-ventilated, over-heated, full of dirt, filth, vermin and stench, and that, consequently, they are in a most unwholesome, health-destroying and disease-breeding condition." The doctor, speaking of one particular case, says: "On the fourth floor I found four very small rooms, occupied by five sewing-machines, twenty-four working hands, and the family of the boss consisting of himself, wife, and five living children. The mother reported to affiant that, within the last few years, six of her children had died of various diseases here in the same place." Relying upon these and other facts, which he relates, the Doctor declares it to be his deliberate conclusion, as a medical man, that "the dust, filth, and dirt, accumulated in the 'sweating dens' he has visited and examined, contain the germs of the prevailing infectious diseases, such as diphtheria, scarlatina, measles, erysipelas, and smallpox, and that the clothing manufactured in these shops is impregnated with such germs, and consequently may transmit and spread the aforesaid diseases to persons who handle and wear it."

These places referred to in this affidavit by Dr. Stiebling, who is a wealthy and respectable medical practitioner, are places where goods are made almost exclusively for Boston houses.

Another physician of standing and repute,

Dr. Markierez, who made an investigation of the sweating district, in connection with a commission from the advisory board of the operative tailors of Boston, in August, 1889, states that the section of New York city in which the tenement-house system of clothing manufacture is carried on, is filthy and infested with vermin; and he further affirms that the sanitary condition of these tenement houses is so low that the death rate is frightful and almost beyond comprehension.

That the sweating system in New York degrades the men and women employed in the sweatshops, may be inferred from the fact that men and women to the number of twelve have been found sleeping together in one of these workrooms. The tenement-house factories are so crowded that no such thing as privacy or modesty, on the part of men or women, is possible; the usual water-closet is a wooden bucket upon every landing, which fills the air with its vile and death-breeding stench.

The New York sweaters, like some of their English prototypes, take advantage of the newly arrived foreigners who do not understand the language. Green hands, who have just arrived at Castle Garden, are pure gold for the contractors. Full-grown men among these will receive, probably, two dollars a week, but one case was discovered where a man was only paid eighty cents for his week's labor. A fourteen-year-old boy was found in a Jewish sweat-shop, who, although he had been in the shop eight months, was still receiving only his board. If that is not slavery, what is it?

But now let us come to Boston. To begin with, I. S. Mullen, State Inspector of factories and workshops, testified, before the committee on public health, of the Massachusetts Legislature, on the 30th of last March, that he had found two places in Boston as bad as anything he had seen in New York. How much that means, you can imagine, after the descriptions I have given.

The State inspectors of factories and public buildings, in their report to Chief Wade of the Massachusetts district police, say that "the confidential clerk of perhaps the largest concern in town assured us that but a small part of their goods were made in New York, and that in shops; that all of their nice work was done in Boston; admitted the fact of tenement-house clothing, but thought the greater part of it was worn in New York, and wished that its manu-

PAUL REVERE HOUSE, NORTH SQUARE.

facture could be prohibited by law. This gentleman, as well as some others questioned, believed that relatively there was as much tenement-house work done in Boston as in New York, and under nearly as unwholesome conditions."

The *Boston Evening Record*, of September 29, 1890, speaks as follows of Boston sweating: "The shops are scattered all over the city proper, and a visit to one is a visit to all. The cheapest shop in the city is on lower Hanover Street. The work is done in a square, low-studded room about twenty-four feet square. Within this space are sixteen women and three men at work. There are also half a dozen sewing-machines, a large stove (kept in full blast to heat the flat-irons, necessary at every stage of clothing manufacture), two pressing-machines, and piles of unfinished clothing. Two windows illumine the room, furnishing light for the nineteen workers. Working hours are from seven A. M. to six P. M., with no clipping of time at either end of the day. The proprietor is a Hebrew. One of the operatives thus describes the life: 'We make from two dollars and a half to four dollars a week, depending on how strong we are, but none of us can make the last figure very long. The air is bad, and the room is kept too hot. In the warm, summer days the heat was something awful. Every little while there is a cut-down, and about once in so often the boss fails, and leaves the girls in the lurch about their pay.

"'Another bad thing is the "sample" game. A small lot of garments are brought in, which, we are told, must be made up very carefully. We are made to rip, and do work over, to suit the notions of the big firms, who want the garments to send out on the road. It takes twice as long to make such a coat, but we get no more for it. Of course the game is played on us when the coats are not really samples. If we accidentally scorch the cloth a little, in pressing, we have to pay for that.'"

An officer of the Operatives' Union puts the number of sweat-shops in Boston at one hundred and fifty, but this does not include the smaller tenement-house shops that are beginning to develop here very rapidly.

I have, myself, visited a number of these shops during the past few weeks. I will describe a few of them very briefly. Here is one in two rooms. There is no light except from the end of the room, which contains twenty-three people, men, women, and little girls. I am satisfied that some of the girls could not have been more than twelve or thirteen. One of the women had a little baby which, though almost entirely naked, was crying from the heat and poisonous air. The place did not look as if it had been swept for weeks. The clothing, both finished and unfinished, was piled up in every direction, and workers walked over it with their sweaty feet, for they wore only such clothing as was absolutely indispensable. The stench of the place was sickening in the extreme.

I went into another place, where there were eighteen men and twelve girls. As near as I could judge, the ages of the girls were from ten to fifteen. The men were nearly all smoking, and that, together with the heat from the fire necessary for the pressing, made an atmosphere that was almost intolerable, even for a few moments. I was not astonished that the girls looked pallid and sickly. There was only one filthy water-closet for men and women.

I was in a little tenement-house Jew shop where a man and four boys were making knee pants in a bedroom. The clothing was piled upon the bed, which was one of the filthiest assortments of tenement-house bedding that I have ever seen -- and that is saying a great deal. The largest shop I visited was one in which there were seventy-nine people employed. They occupied four rooms. The rooms were quite large, but were filthy almost beyond description. The coal was piled up in huge heaps

REAR OF NORTH END TENEMENT HOUSE.

on the floor; ashes, both in barrels and heaps, were scattered about; clothing was flung over the floors everywhere; dirt and scraps of cloth literally made a carpet for these rooms. These seventy-nine people were about evenly divided between the sexes, and yet for all this herd of humanity there was only one water-closet, the door of which stood open, on the landing, and the poisonous stench filled all the rooms; the floor about it was damp and filthy. How any woman or girl could work in this shop, and retain her self-respect, I do not understand. I estimated that at least twenty boys and girls of this company were under fifteen; one little boy sitting on the floor hard at work was almost crying with a headache. The men were smoking cigarettes here, as in other places, and this added to the poisonous condition of the air. The majority of these people could not speak English. Taken altogether, they were a hopeless-looking lot. Many of them had a brutal, hunted look in their faces.

Remember, this is not Glasgow, or London, or New York, but in the heart of Boston, in the month of June, 1891. It is easy to say that these people are foreigners, and that they had poor wages where they came from; that they are probably as well off here as they were at home, and that they are too ignorant and brutal to suffer, as more refined and cultivated people would. Putting all other questions aside for a moment, let us remember that these people are setting up a standard of living in our midst, which, if permitted to become established, will dictate its cruel laws to all the laboring people in the community.

COMMONWEALTH AVENUE.

If this system is allowed to go on, there are people living in luxury, who are indifferently pooh-poohing this whole question, whose grandchildren will be starved to death in a sweat-shop.

No investment exacts such cruel usury as indifference to injustice. A wrong, uncared for in a North End tenement house will avenge itself, sooner or later, on Beacon Hill or Commonwealth Avenue.

I thank God for every indication of discontent, on the part of laboring men and women, at conditions which cramp or fetter the free utterance of their manhood or womanly glory. In that divine discontent is the hope of the race. Our own Lowell sings: —

> "The hope of truth grows stronger day by day.
> I hear the soul of man around me waking,
> Like a great sea its frozen fetters breaking,
> And flinging up to heaven its sunlit spray,
> Tossing huge continents in scornful play,
> And crushing them with din of grinding thunder
> That makes old emptinesses stare in wonder.
> The memory of a glory passed away
> Lingers in every heart, as in the shell
> Resounds the by-gone freedom of the sea.
> And every hour new signs of promise tell
> That the great soul shall once again be free;
> For high and yet more high the murmurs swell
> Of inward strife for truth and liberty."

V

THE RELATION OF WAGES TO MORALS

"When the toiler's heart you clutch,
　　Conscience is not valued much;
　He recks not a bloody smutch
　　　On his gold;
　Everything to you he defers,
　You are potent reasoners;
　At your whisper Treason stirs,
　　　Hunger and Cold!"
　　　　　　JAMES RUSSELL LOWELL.

V.

THE RELATION OF WAGES TO MORALS

WHEN Henry W. Grady, the brilliant Southern orator, was in Boston on his last visit, only a few weeks before his sad and untimely death, he charmed us all by his entrancing word-picture of a happy country home. The fields, the lowing kine, the well-appointed farmhouse, the noble farmer, the contented matron, the dutiful children, the hospitable welcome of their guest, the cheerful and reverent evening worship — all these and more stand out on the glowing canvas under his words, as I have myself seen them in real life a thousand times. About such a home, and the toilers that support it, there is a halo of glory. There is, however, a great deal said about the dignity of labor which is nothing more than oratorical commonplace — the meaningless froth of the rhetorician. There is no dignity about labor in itself. What is there about piling bricks on top of each other, or mixing mortar, or sewing blue denim into overalls, or trading earthen jars for nickel coin, that has about it any inherent dignity? It is only as there is mixed with the mortar, or builded with the bricks, the holy cement of a moral purpose; only as there is stitched into the cloth the diviner thread of hopeful love; only as the deed gathers the aroma of an aspiring human life, is it a dignified transaction. But when you make of the laborer a slave, degrade his work to a mere fight for bread, harass him by continual debt, put him in a vile tenement house that smothers all holy ambition, labor has no longer dignity, it smells rather of the dungeon and the pit.

Honest labor, continued through reasonable hours, paid at a rate which assures a wholesome support, is ennobling; but overwork, that is hopeless of comfortable reward, is degrading in the extreme. On the continent of Europe, where men and women work in the factories for fourteen and sixteen hours in a day, the laborers are reduced simply to machines. They have a wooden look, when you meet them on the streets, that is startling to an American observer. Every observant European travelling in this country notices the difference in the in-

DRYING "THE FIND."

telligence of the average countenance of American working-people, both among men and women. But how long can we expect that to last if the dominion of the sweater is to spread in our midst? Reduce wages to the point where the laborer has to either remain at the shop or take his work home and work into the night, and drive it on through Sunday as well, and you simply brutalize the workman.

It is idle, and pharisaical as well, for us to shrug our shoulders and say this is not a question for the pulpit. So intimate is the relation between the body and the soul, that every question which has to do with the feeding or clothing of a human body is, at the last analysis, a moral question. The great generals of history have understood that the moral force of their armies depended largely upon the provision wagon. Frederick the Great once wrote: "Where one desires a solid basis for the good organization of an army, it is necessary to have regard to the stomach." Napoleon once said: "The soldier has his heart in his abdomen;" and Von Moltke adds his testimony: "In a campaign no food is costly except that which is bad."

One of the greatest of physiologists, Moleschott, says: "Courage, readiness, and activity depend in a great measure upon a healthy and abundant nourishment. Hunger makes heart and head empty. No force of will can make up for an impoverished blood, a badly nourished muscle, or an exhausted nerve." All these tend to the one conclusion, that the moral and intellectual life is very largely subject to physiological conditions. A man, of course, may be a scoundrel and well-fed; but, on the other hand, poor food and undue exposure to cold and heat have tremendous influence in breaking down the resistance-power against temptation to evil. Courage is the safeguard both of truth and honesty.

Break down a man's courage by overwork, bad food, and poisonous air, and you have opened the way for lying, theft, and a whole brood of vicious tendencies. You may find this strongly illustrated in Hugo's story of Jean Valjean, who in his despair begins his criminal career by stealing a loaf of bread to keep his sister's children from starving.

We get so in the habit of thinking of drunkenness as the chief cause of poverty, as it undoubtedly is, — for when a man drinks to excess his whole character falls to pieces like a child's house of cards, — that we forget, or fail to perceive, the companion fact, that poverty is, in turn, a great and serious factor in the spread of drunkenness.

When a man or woman is physically exhausted, there is a natural craving for stimulant, and the power of resistance is reduced to the lowest point, if not to zero. It will not do for us to forget that the drink habit is often a symptom of exhaustion. Here are a man and a woman who receive such low wages that they are driven into unhealthy quarters. They ought to have four or five rooms in order to the least approach to wholesome living; but poverty herds them in two, or it may be only one, for within the past month I have myself seen many families of father and mother and as many as five children packed into one little room, in one case only seven by nine feet. The air is poisonous; and, after the rent is paid, the food-money is insufficient, and sickness is the result. I do not mean that large numbers of people in Boston are literally starved to death for lack of bread; but I do mean that thousands of men and women and children in this city are compelled to eat such a quality of food that the result is a condition of mind and body which is subject to an unsatiable thirst for strong drink, and makes drunkards of those who would otherwise be sober people.

In company with two gentlemen I was examining a filthy court a few weeks ago, when, in the rear of a bake-shop under a shed, we noticed some curious machinery, and were looking at it rather inquisitively when a young lad came up out of the bakery in the cellar, and, in answer to our inquiries, said in a matter-of-course way that it was a mill for grinding old bread and stale crackers into flour, which was again baked into a cheaper class of bread. This grade of flour may make a very nourishing food, but the incident left a most unpleasant taste in my mouth.

It is a commonplace thing, I know, to say that the American home is the strongest fortress of our civilization. It is one of those things, however, that needs to be said over and over again. Before the church or the state there must be the home. Destroy that, and the whole fabric of our civilization will come crashing to the ground in a common ruin. But the reduction of wages below the comfort point means, inevitably, the deterioration of the home. The father and mother and the children must know each other, if the home is to be welded together with mutual love. Acquaintance of that character, however, requires that

THE NORTH END MISSION.

they shall be together under such conditions that they may come to enjoy the gifts and talents that each possess. But wages are being reduced to the point where the home is only a sleeping-barrack and a lunch-counter for supper and breakfast. Remember that poor wages mean long hours; and long hours that exhaust all the energy of the laborer mean ignorance; and ignorance, when it is finished, means immorality.

There is only about so much vital force in the average human being. If all this force is put into one's daily toil, there is none left for helpful conversation, for sympathetic communion at home, for uplifting reading, or for worship. Persevere in that course, and you reach barbarism: the road faces that way.

Insufficient wages have their relation to the demoralization of laboring-people in many ways that are not perceived by people who look no deeper than the surface. The city abounds in organized firms of sharpers who prey upon the necessities of the hard-pinched laborer. If you will examine a copy of "The Banker and Tradesman," published in this city, and look down the column of chattel-mortgages, for any week, you will see a very innocent-appearing column, to the unadvised, but one that is full of devilish wickedness to a man who has been behind the scenes. If there be anything in Boston that can rival the cruelty of the tenement-house sweat-shop, you will find it in the dens of some chattel-mortgage sharks, whose business methods I have investigated. Here is a woman who made her living by making overalls at five cents a pair. Times, of course, were always hard with her. Her husband was out of work a good part of the time. At a period when they were in a specially hard place, they borrowed ten dollars of one of these human sharks. They were to pay two dollars a month interest on it. If at any time it ran over two or three days and the interest was not paid, so that the collector had to call for it, he charged and collected two dollars extra for calling. I should have stated that this money was secured by a chattel-mortgage upon every article of household furniture they possessed. These mortgages are ironclad, and put the people at the mercy of the man who holds them. In the course of fifteen months, under cover of this loan of ten dollars, this firm managed to squeeze forty dollars out of the hard earnings of these people; and then they came to foreclose the mortgage and take away the furniture, and would have removed every household article they possessed, had not the police-officer on the beat, a man of noble heart and generous instincts, stepped in and agreed to be responsible personally for the amount. Here is another case, all of the papers of which are now in my my hands: A man and his wife borrowed twenty dollars; the firm charged two dollars for making out the papers, so that the note read twenty-two dollars. The agent called on them once, and charged two dollars for that. In the course of ten months they paid twenty dollars interest. The matter then came to the attention of the secretary of a charitable association, who forced the brokers to settle up the case for six dollars. I know of another case of a Swede family who "got behind," and could not pay the rent. Sickness came upon them, and they borrowed fifty dollars. In a little over a year they paid sixty dollars interest, but the principal had not been reduced a dollar.

Some of the instalment firms are just as bad, and many times are in league with these sharpers. A case has come to my knowledge where a man with a wife and family of five children bought furniture amounting to a hundred and thirty-five dollars. After he had paid seventy dollars, he was taken sick and had to go to the hospital. The wife was unable to meet the instalments promptly, and the firm threatened to take away her furniture. She asked the agent of a charitable organization to intercede for her. This gentleman wrote to the firm and begged them to postpone their foreclosure, and mercifully give the poor family a little more time. But this they absolutely refused to do, and came in the midst of the raw winds of March, and took all the household furniture away, including the stove and the loaf of bread in the oven. These are not hearsay stories, but facts that can be proved by undoubted evidence.

Women are the greatest sufferers from depreciation of wages. Commissioner Carroll Wright's report on the working-women in great cities, given to the public two years since, contains some interesting facts. The investigation on which the report is based covered twenty-two of the larger cities of the United States, and three hundred and forty-two distinct industries, excluding the professional and semi-professional callings, such as teaching, stenography, typewriting, and telegraphy. The total number of women individually interviewed was 17,427.

This is only six or seven per cent of the whole number of women engaged in the class of work indicated, but the Commissioner declares that the investigation is representative so far as the number of women whose affairs enter into it is to be considered. The average age of the women is given as twenty-two years and seven months, though the concentration is greatest at the age of eighteen. . . . The general average at the beginning of work is put at fifteen years and four months.

A great majority of the women interviewed are single, and the average weekly earnings for the cities, as a whole, are five dollars and twenty-four cents. Take your pencil and count it up — room-rent, board, and clothing — and see how much you have left for books or music, recreation or religion.

The twentieth annual report of the Massachusetts Bureau of Labor Statistics for last year shows not only the poor pay of women, but the cruel and unjust disparity of wages between men and women doing the same work. Beginning with the lowest rate of wages, for the first comparison of relative male and female pay, it appears that of actual wages paid to 248,200 employés of both sexes, 8.99 per cent of all males receive less than five dollars a week, 4.85 per cent less than six dollars, and 6.77 per cent less than seven dollars. That is, about 20 per cent of all males average less than one dollar per day. But the females working at this low scale of wages comprise 72.94 per cent of all the workers. In the higher scale of wages, 63.78 per cent of all the males receive a dollar and a half or more per day. But only a little more than 10 per cent of the females employed are paid wages as high. Out of 7,257 receiving twenty dollars a week and over, only 268 are women. But the cruelest part of all this is that women, standing side by side with men in the same shops and stores, are paid far less wages for the same work. This is an aristocracy of sex that shames and belies all our claims to democracy.

This injustice in the wages of women is already beginning to bear a fearful fruitage.

Miss Alice S. Woodbridge, the secretary of the Working-women's Society of New York, after a recent tour of investigation, sums up the result of her observations in the following words: "The wages paid to women average between four and four and one-half dollars per week, and are often reduced by unreasonable and excessive fines. The little cash-girls do not average two dollars a week. In one large house the average wages for saleswomen and cash-girls is two dollars and forty cents a week. In many fashionable houses the saleswomen are not allowed to leave the counter between the hours of eleven A. M. and three P. M., except for lunch, and if a saleswoman has a customer when the lunch-hour arrives, she is obliged to remain and wait on the customer, and the time so consumed is deducted from lunch-time.

"If mistakes are made, they are charged to the saleswomen and cash-girls. Generally, the goods are placed in a bin and slide down to the floor below. If a check is lost, the goods are charged to the saleswoman, though it may be the fault of the shipping-clerk. In some stores the fines are divided between the superintendent and the time-keeper. In one store where these fines amounted to three thousand dollars, the superintendent was heard to reproach the time-keeper with not being strict enough. Men's wages are very low," says Miss Woodbridge, " but it seems that they can not fall below the point where existence is possible. Women's wages, however, have no low limit, since the paths of shame are always open to them. Cases might be cited where frail, delicate women, unable to exist on the salaries they earn, are forced to crime or suicide. The story of Mrs. Henderson, who threw herself from the attic window of a lodging-house some time ago, is the story of many another.

"There have been many such instances in the last two weeks. Mrs. Henderson could not live on the salaries offered her. She could live if she accepted the 'propositions' of her employers. The hope of an easier life, the fear of death, and the natural clinging to life, turn many working-women into the paths of shame." Miss Woodbridge further adds that " in Paris it is an understood fact that women who are employed in shops cannot exist without assistance from other questionable sources, and," she continues, "unless something is done at once, this must also become the case in our land, where we pride ourselves on our respect for honest toil."

Helen Campbell, in her "Prisoners of Poverty," opens a little window into the terrible temptation which comes to generous young souls under this pressure of unrequited toil. In her true story of Rose Haggerty, who was sewing her very life into the support of her orphan brothers and sisters, we have a practical illustration of the results of this injustice. "There came a Saturday night when she took her bundle of work, — shirts again, and now eighty-five cents a dozen [it is worse than that under some of our Boston sweaters]; there were five dozen, and when the dollar and a half was laid away for rent, it was easy to see what was left for food, coal, and light. Clothing had ceased to be a part of the question. The children were barefoot. They had a bit of meat on Sunday; but for the rest, bread, potatoes, and tea were the diet, with cabbage and a bit of pork, now and then, for luxuries.

"Nora (a little sick sister) had been failing, and to-night Rose planned to buy her 'something with a taste to it,' and looked at the sausages hanging in long links with a sudden reckless determination to get enough for all. She was faint with hunger, and staggered as she passed a basement restaurant, from which came savory smells, snuffed longingly by some half-starved children. Her turn was long in coming; and as she laid her bundle on the counter, she saw suddenly that her needle had 'jumped,' and that half an inch or so of band required resewing. As she looked, the foreman's knife slipped under the place, and in a moment half the band had been ripped. 'That's no good,' he said. 'You are getting botchier all the time.' 'Give it to me,' Rose pleaded. 'I'll do it over.' 'Take it if you like,' he said indifferently, ' but there is no pay for that kind o' work.' He had counted her money as he spoke, and Rose cried out as she saw the sum: 'Do you mean you will cheat me of the whole dozen, because half an inch on one has gone wrong?' 'Call it what you like,' he said. 'R. & Co. ain't going to send out anything but first-class work. Stand out of the way and let the next have a chance. There's your three dollars and forty cents.'

"Rose went out silently, choking down rash words that would have lost her work altogether; but as she left the dark stairs, and felt again the cutting wind from the river, she stood still, something more than despair on her face. The children could hardly fare worse without her than with her. The river could not be colder than this cold world that gave her no chance, and that had no place for anything but rascals.

"She turned toward it as the thought came; but some one had her arm, and she cried out suddenly, and tried to wrench away. 'Easy now,' a voice said. 'You're breakin' your heart for trouble, an' here I am in the nick o' time. Come with me an' you'll have no more of it, for my pocket's full to-night, and that's more than it'll be in the mornin' if you do n' take me in tow.' It was a sailor from a merchantman just in, and Rose looked at him for a moment. Then she took his arm and walked toward Roosevelt Street. It might be dishonor, but it was certainly food and warmth for the children, and what did it matter? She had fought her fight for twenty years, and it had been a vain

A BOSTON "BRIDGE OF SIGHS."

struggle." When she poured her heart-breaking story into Helen Campbell's ears, she said,

"Let God Almighty judge who's to blame most — I that was driven, or them that drove me to the pass I'm in."

Ah! but you say, even as you sigh over this fearful picture, "That is in wicked New York." Yes, but Boston has its tragedies equally as heartrending and shameful. During this past week a thoroughly respectable young married woman, whose evidence is indisputable, and who, prior to her marriage, had worked for several years as a saleswoman in the Boston stores, told me that at one time her employer told her that, on account of the dull season, he would have to discharge her, but that he would give her a good recommendation, and if she would take it to another prominent dry-goods house, which he named, he thought she would at once secure employment. She took the letter of commendation, and went as directed. The employing agent of the firm to which she was sent asked her how much salary she had been receiving, and she answered, "Five dollars a week." He replied, "I cannot pay you that much, I can only give you three dollars a week;" to which she answered, "I can hardly live on what I have now, and I could not possibly live on three dollars a week." He replied, with an insulting and meaning smile, "You would have to depend on the outside friend for that." She looked him in the eye, and said, "I want to earn an honest living, and I don't want any outside friend," and at that walked away. She told her employer of her reception; and he said he did not intend to discharge her, but had heard that this firm was in the habit of doing that sort of thing, and was determined to find out if it were true.

I received a letter from a gentleman in Conway, N. H., this week, who writes, not knowing that I was intending to discuss this question: "After you have given the sweating-system one round, can you not take up the question of the girls working in the big stores? I have just heard a well-authenticated account of a man high in authority in one of the largest stores, suggesting the way to ruin to a young girl from the country, who said, when she learned what her wages were to be, that they would not be sufficient to give her a bare support. This not only shows the attitude of these wealthy merchants to the souls of their working-girls, but it shows that they are conscious of their attitude, and have deliberately chosen to take it." I am told, upon undoubtedly credible testimony, that another young woman who came to Boston from the country, and sought work in several stores, was so outraged at the vile suggestions which were made to her about means of adding to her salary, that she went back to the house of her friend, — a lady of as high standing as any in the city, — and cried and sobbed all night long. She said she would beg or starve before she would submit herself to such outrage again.

It is impossible to turn these incidents aside as exaggerations. They are horrible, I know; but the most horrible thing about them is, that they are true. You will say perhaps, as some have said during the past few weeks of my exposure of the sweat-shops, "What good will it all do, this harrowing of people's minds with these cruel stories?"

I do not know how much good will be done. I only know that I could not retain my self-respect and keep silent.

Nothing is more foolish than for us to keep still, hoping that in some way these wrongs will remedy themselves. Shall we look to the sweater, the chattel-mortgage shark, the lecherous merchant, to reform themselves? They do not care how long, nor at what a pittance, men and women work, or to what fearful extremities they are driven. Reforms will never come from the gold-box of Mammon. We must cry aloud and spare not until these devilish cruelties and unblushing crimes are impossible in our fair city.

The words of the Christ, as interpreted by James Russell Lowell, are ringing in my ears:—

> "With gates of silver and bars of gold,
> Ye have fenced my sheep from their father's fold.
> I have heard the dropping of their tears
> In heaven these eighteen hundred years."

Then if we reply with the selfish assurance of some of these pharisaical political economists who are criticising me to-day:—

> "O Lord and Master, not ours the guilt,
> We build but as our fathers built;
> Behold Thine images, how they stand,
> Sovereign and sole, through all the land."

How his answer will put us to shame and confusion : —

> "Then Christ sought out an artisan,
> A low-browed, stunted, haggard man,
> And a motherless girl, whose fingers thin,
> Pushed from her faintly want and sin.
>
> These set He in the midst of them,
> And as they drew back their garment-hem,
> For fear of defilement, 'Lo here,' said He,
> 'The IMAGES ye have made of Me!'"

VI

THE WAGES AND TEMPTATIONS OF WORKING-PEOPLE

"Face to face with shame and insult
 Since she drew her baby breath,
Were it strange to find her knocking
 At the cruel door of death ?
Were it strange if she should parley
 With the great arch fiend of sin ?"

   ALICE CARY : *The Edge of Doom.*

VI

THE WAGES AND TEMPTATIONS OF WORKING-PEOPLE

I HAVE been asked to give a reason for the faith that is in me in regard to certain painful charges made by me in a recent sermon on Wages and Morals — to the effect that the persons high in authority in some respectable Boston stores regard favorably immoral relations on the part of the employés, in order to make it possible for them to live on the slender wages paid them.

Without repeating here any of the cases mentioned in my sermon, which has had considerable publicity through the daily press, permit me to quote Mr. Henry Chase, agent of the Society for the Prevention of Crime. He says that in conversation with a leading Boston merchant, the merchant said plainly that he had every reason to believe that some of the men working in his store paid the room-rent and a trifling sum besides to working-girls, and lived with them regularly. Another Boston merchant said to Mr. Chase that he regarded that kind of life on the part of his clerks favorably; that the wages these young men received made it impossible for them to marry and support a wife.

I am informed of another case, upon perfectly credible authority, of two young women, strangers in the city, who applied to a leading store for a situation and were offered work, but when informed of the wages they were to receive, exclaimed, "How could we live on such wages as that?" The employment agent of the house replied, "It is presumed you will have a gentleman friend to assist you." The girls looked at him dumfounded for a moment; and when his meaning dawned upon the one who had acted as spokesman, she burst into tears and they hurried from the store. Only the dread of bringing unpleasant notoriety to these thoroughly respectable young women saved this scoundrel from a horsewhipping at the hands of their indignant male relatives.

A leading Boston lady of wealth and social standing, writing to thank me for calling public attention to the subject, says that she herself knew of a girl who was told to "'look to her gentleman friends' for the means to eke out a bare livelihood supplied by her wages in a prominent store;" and adds: "Such things are outrageous, and it is well you are making them known." I have within the past week received another letter from the president of the W. C. T. U. in one of the Boston wards, a lady who has had more than twenty-five years' experience in practical reform work in this city. She says: "I have just read in my *Congregationalist* the reference to your sermon of last Sunday on the officials in two of our large Boston stores suggesting immoral means of eking out their scanty wages to their employés. I want to thank you for presenting this terrible wickedness existing among us, and if the extent could only be known, every white-ribbon woman in Boston would boycott those stores. I could call names of splendid young women, thrown on their own resources, applying for situations, who were cursed, as we might say, with a good face and a fine figure, fairly insulted with offers made. More young girls have been ruined in that way than in any other. In sheer desperation, not even earning enough to pay the rent of a mean attic and keep hunger away, to say nothing of clothing and other things, they have, after spending the last cent, and not having anything to take them home, resorted to the last means."

This is a terrible letter — terribly true. I could go on, column after column, with these details. "But," the critic says, "why don't you name these firms, and put them in the pillory of public contempt?" I can tell you why in a few words. You cannot name the firms without giving the name of the young woman thus wickedly approached; and to name any young woman in such a connection, no matter how innocent or pure she is, is to put a mark upon her as long as she lives.

No woman is willing to run that gantlet; and so, in the very nature of the case, it would rarely happen that you could publicly punish the guilty party. "Well, then," says the critic, "you would better hold your peace." Let us consider that a moment. If a burglary has been committed in town, do you keep silent until you are prepared to name the burglar and publicly indict him for trial? No, indeed. You tell all the neighbors, and publish in all the newspapers, that such a house has been invaded, that burglars are in town. What is the good of doing this? Why, any school-boy knows that it is a blessing to every other householder in the town. It puts people on their guard, and calls special attention to their bolts and locks. If there is any good reason why we should not follow the same common-sense course in this matter under consideration, I do not know what it is.

I do not bring a broad, sweeping accusation against either class of persons especially concerned in this article. I am no defamer of my kind. I believe that the majority of Boston merchants are honest, pure-minded men. I believe that the majority of Boston working-women, old or young, are as pure and noble as any women in the world. Nevertheless, I have stated in this article undeniable facts — facts which I can substantiate to the satisfaction of any honest man or woman who, still doubting, cares to see me personally about the matter. These facts are serious enough to give us all reason for solemn and earnest reflection.

VII

BOSTON'S UNCLE TOM'S CABIN

"That each should in his house abide,
Therefore was the world so wide."

    RALPH WALDO EMERSON : *Fragments
     of Nature and Life.*

VII

BOSTON'S UNCLE TOM'S CABIN

WHEN, over one-half of our land, there hung the black pall of African slavery, no other one thing, perhaps, did more to reveal the terrible cruelty of the system, and to arouse the indignation of the civilized world, than Harriet Beecher Stowe's "Uncle Tom's Cabin."

In June, 1882, when the *élite* of American literature gathered at Boston to celebrate her seventieth birthday, Dr. Oliver Wendell Holmes read a poem in which Mrs. Stowe's share in the emancipation of the colored race was recorded with equal wit and pathos: —

> "When Archimedes so long ago
> Spoke out so grandly, '*Dos pou sto* —
> Give me a place to stand on;
> I'll move your planet for you now,'
> He little dreamed or fancied how
> The *sto* at last should find its *pou*
> For woman's faith to land on.

> Her lever was the wand of art,
> Her fulcrum was the human heart,
>   Whence all unfailing aid is;
> She moved the earth, its thunders pealed,
> Its mountains shook, its temples reeled,
> The blood-red fountains were unsealed,
>   And Moloch sunk to Hades."

Mrs. Stowe, in the preface of her son's biography of herself, aptly quotes the words of Mr. Valiant-for-Truth in the "Pilgrim's Progress:" "My sword I give to him that shall succeed me in my pilgrimage, and my courage and skill to him that can get it." May God grant us courage and skill to use the memory of "Uncle Tom's Cabin" to serve the "white slaves" of our own time and city!

To begin by quoting from Mrs. Stowe's famous story: "The cabin of Uncle Tom was a small log building close adjoining to 'the house,' as the negro *par excellence* designates his master's dwelling. In front it had a neat garden-patch where every summer strawberries, raspberries, and a variety of fruits and vegetables flourished under careful training." This little log house was a small and crowded dwelling-place for Uncle Tom and his wife and little ones, yet it had several things in its favor. In the first place it had plenty of sunshine and pure air. It was an individual cabin, occupied by Uncle Tom's family alone. The climate was sunshiny; and when Uncle Tom's wife, Aunt Chloe, wanted to wash, she could build a fire out in the open air, and spread her clothing on the fragrant raspberry-bushes, while her woolly-headed little flock were sent scampering over the pastures and fields.

Now let us look at the Boston cabins. In the first place, there are no individual cabins for the poor. The price of land makes that impossible. A big Boston tenement house means from four to ten cabins on a floor, and from three to six floors under one roof. In a great many of these sunlight is an impossibility. Boston is peculiarly cursed with the rear tenement. All through the North End and some parts of the West End and "the Cove," there abound dark courts, oftentimes reached only by a tunnel, that are almost entirely barren of the sunlight. For instance, there is a court off North Street, reached by a tunnel such as I have described, where the tenement houses are three deep from the street.

The inside tenement, facing on the court, through most of the year is densely packed with people.

COURT OFF NORTH STREET.

For a large part of the length of the court it is only four feet wide, and the front windows of the house, which is three stories in height, look out on the dark wall which is only four feet away. On a dark day there is scarcely any light at all in these rooms; and on the brightest sunshiny day there is only a little light during the middle of the day, and never any direct rays of the sun. I found, up in one of these rooms, a young woman with her first-born in her arms, — a pale, sickly little child, not yet a year old, that will certainly die before the summer is out, if it stays there. This poor young mother was born in Maine, and followed her husband down here from the green fields and the breath of the pines. The husband works out of the city during the day, coming home late in the evening and going out in the morning; but all day long the mother and wife is kept here with her invalid child. Their faces look like potato-vines that have sprouted and grown in the cellar. They are dying for the lack of sunshine and pure air.

Modern science is imperative in its urgent emphasis on the influence of light and sunshine on health; and we are told that children brought up even in close valleys do not thrive so well as those raised on the hillsides or the tablelands, and that families through the generations grow smaller in stature, and less vigorous in physical and mental force, if much excluded from light and sunshine. He was a wise old father who lived out on the plains, and came to visit his son, who had moved into a deep mountain gorge. At family prayers he thanked the Lord that his son was still well, although he lived where the sun rose at nine o'clock in the morning and set at four in the afternoon. But there are scores of Boston tenement houses where the sun never rises at all, except on the roof-tops, or now and then sends a slant ray, thrown down into the dark court in seeming mockery. It is impossible for any one to get from language alone, either spoken or written, an adequate idea of the loneliness, the sense of gloom, the filth and squalor, of the apartments in some of these Boston tenement houses. It requires a strong stomach, and a still stronger determination that nothing shall thwart you from knowing how your brothers and sisters live, to take you the second time into such a place. Go with me into one that is not ten minutes' walk from the mansions of wealth and

luxury on Beacon Hill. We go back through a narrow passage, where you can touch the walls on either side of you, and then down some steps into a dark underground court. Now you have to bend over almost double till you feel your way to a door on your left, and knock. In answer to the "Come," you open the door and go in, and are barely able to stand upright inside the room. We are in a cellar about ten feet square, and this is separated from others like it by a partition. We are really in one room of a big cellar stretching under a crowded tenement house over our heads. We look around us; and as soon as our eyes get accustomed to the darkness — for the only light is from the narrow width of glass, reaching from the ground up to the floor which forms the ceiling of the room where we stand — we see that this is the den — for you cannot call it anything else — of an old man and his wife. They have both passed threescore. Their locks are white, and they are no longer able to work as hard as formerly.

They have had children, but they are dead. The two old people, waifs from bonny Scotland, have probably made their last move, until the city sends around its rough box and dead-cart to take them to their last sleep in the Potter's Field. They used to live up-stairs; but as they grew older, and were not so spry as formerly, they could no longer pay the rent, and therefore moved down till at last they are at the bottom. For this den of misery, in which a well-to-do Western farmer would not think of keeping his hog, they pay one dollar per week. They have to cook, eat, sleep, and do everything else pertaining to domestic life, in this one dark, filthy hole. The combination of smells is indescribable. But as you begin to sicken and are ready to flee, you remember, with a shock, that what sickens you so in five minutes this old white-headed man and his wife have to endure day after day, and night after night, and on — and on — there is no hope of anything better this side of a pauper's grave. Don't blame these old people for not keeping their den clean. Nobody could keep it clean. There is no sunshine, and only a little while in the day any light at all. It is necessarily damp and mouldy. We talk with the old man. He goes fishing and does such odd jobs as he is able. He says

SICK MAN IN UNDERGROUND APARTMENT.

one of the worst things with which they have to contend is the rats; and then he points out places in the wall, down next to the ground, that he has filled with little billets of wood, stuck in every-which-way, in his efforts to keep the rats from preying on them at night. Let us foot up the column.

Old age, with its accompanying weakness and loss of hopefulness and courage; darkness, with the brooding sense of gloom and melancholy that goes with it; noisome smells, that make even a breath of the narrow, crowded street seem like a draught from Paradise; filth, mould, and rats that compete with you for what really has been taken from their appropriate domain, — and yet remember that down there, in all that, and more, for no tongue or pen can tell its wretchedness, live hundreds of your brothers and sisters. Not the drunken and the dissolute only, for about this place which I have described, or its tenants, there was not the slightest suggestion of liquor anywhere.

Down on North Street is an old house which, the traditions tell us, was originally built for a " wayside inn," in the good old days before the word hotel was so well known as now. It is not a very large house, as tenement houses go, yet the missionary who is with me assures me that he has found as many as thirty families stowed away under its roof. A wall is built up around the rear and on one side, corralling a little breathing-space or side yard. A stable for two horses comes out of this space; and the stench from these stalls mingles with the stench of the water-closets which are all situated in this yard, and the united fumes rise to every rear window of the establishment.

The stairways are rickety and filthy. We go in at two places to sample the tenantry. In the first we find an old Irish woman who lives here with her two boys. She keeps house for them in two little rooms. Everything is poverty-stricken and dirty. The poor old woman is a wreck in body and in mind. She has buried seven daughters. She says, "I've buried a good flock. Too much trouble broke my very life out of me." We go in at another door. Here is an English woman; she has two children and keeps a boarder. She scrubs now in a bank building, and washes at other places. She sewed for a long time. At first she was paid fourteen cents a pair for finishing pants, then thirteen cents, then twelve cents, and finally ten cents, and then, as it was impossible to get bread for her children on what she could earn, she went to scrubbing. Being a very rugged woman physically, she is able to do this. If she had been frail and delicate, with a young babe, she would have been compelled to keep on finishing pants at ten cents a pair.

It is hot and dirty here everywhere. How could it be otherwise? Every one of these housekeepers must have a fire in her room every time she wants hot water for washing or any other purpose. Take the day of my visit, — one of the hottest in June; it is ninety degrees in the shade, but with the fire in the rickety stove in the room in which this mother and her little girl are working, it cannot be less than a hundred and thirty. But the fire cannot go out, or the washing will stop, and there will be no food to-morrow. For these two miserable sweat-boxes — the paper half torn off, bed-bug dens that nothing could thoroughly cleanse except a fire that would exterminate the very walls — she pays two dollars and a half per week. As a striking illustration of the good results of agitation on these subjects, I called at this house during the past week,

AN ANCIENT TENEMENT.

when one of the tenants told me that my repeated visits to the place, and the fact that I had had a photographer there making views of it, had awakened so much comment in the section that the landlord had got frightened and had had the corridors washed, and had put new paper on some of the rooms.

Off Norman Street in the West End is a court which I have visited during the past week in company with two other gentlemen. The houses on this court are occupied by Italian fruit-venders for the most part.

The court itself is littered up with refuse and decayed fruit in a most filthy and unhealthy manner. In one of these large tenement houses there is no family which occupies more than one room. Let us investigate a few of them. Here is a room fifteen feet long. At its narrow end it is only five feet six inches wide, and at the other end not quite seven feet wide. In this narrow lane five people live. Huge strings of bananas in every stage of ripening hang over the piles of filthy bedding. It is in the second story, and the corridor in front, which is forty-three inches wide — unusually spacious, as you will see later — is half taken up with boxes of decaying fruit, buckets of slops, and piles of refuse. The walls are as black and rusty as the stove.

Here is another family residence in this

building. The size is ten and one-half by ten and one-fourth feet. Four people live here. The entire furnishings are not worth five dollars. The cupboard is a lemon-box with a partition in it, set on the floor. The bread, kneaded and ready to bake, is laid out on an old, dirty, colored handkerchief on the pile of bedding; there are no chairs, table, or other furniture of any kind. Another room which also answers for home for four people, is sixteen feet long and six feet five inches wide. The walls here, as in many other rooms, have large sections of the plastering torn off, and are blackened with many years of smoke and dirt.

The next family we visit has three people. The room is seven by nine feet. The bed covers all except thirty-one inches on one end, and twenty-four inches on one side. There are boxes of fruit under the bed, some of it decaying; what is too rotten to sell must serve for home consumption. And so we go on, room after room, and floor after floor. Now, section fourteen of the law in regard to tenement houses says: " The tenant of any lodging-house or tenement house shall thoroughly cleanse all the rooms, floors, windows, and doors of the house, or part of the house, of which he is the tenant, to the satisfaction of the Board of Health; and the owner or lessee shall well and

ITALIAN FRUIT-VENDERS AT HOME.

sufficiently, to the satisfaction of said board, whitewash and otherwise cleanse the walls and ceilings thereof, once at least in *every year*, in the months of April or May, and have the privies, drains, and cesspools kept in good order, and the passages and stairs kept clean and in good condition."

Now, I have no desire or intention to do any injustice to the members of the Board of Health. They may be over-worked, and have an insufficient force to pay proper attention to their duties; but I state only the simple fact — and I am sure it is a fact that the people generally ought to know — when I say that there is a shameful and dangerous lack of such attention in many of these tenement houses. In regard to the houses I have just described the law is a dead letter. The passages and stairs are filthy beyond description. Some of these corridors are only twenty, twenty-three, and twenty-nine inches wide, and yet, dark and narrow as they are, they are largely filled up with piles of refuse and garbage. In one of these buildings the water-closet on the landing has had the door taken down and put away, so that it stands open day and night.

On some of the walls of these living rooms the cockroaches and bed-bugs swarm in abundance, literally by hundreds, at ten o'clock in the morning. The walls and ceilings have not only *not* been cleansed or whitened this year, but it must have been many years since there has been an attempt made to clean them. In one of these bedrooms I counted twenty-five

COCKROACHES BY FLASH-LIGHT.

boxes of lemons, besides great bunches of half-ripened bananas. Live chickens were kept under the bed in one of these rooms. The fruit which is ripened in these places is sold daily in every section of the city, and people who live with healthful surroundings, far away from this pestilent hole, are risking the health of themselves and their children, unwittingly, by purchasing fruit that cannot help but have absorbed something of the poison from the

BANANA SELLER.

atmosphere of these filthy, crowded quarters. The Board of Health know about this place, for their sign is put up over the doors of these rooms, telling how many are allowed to sleep in each room; but they might as well have kept the sign in the office for all the good it has done, for in nearly every room the inmates admitted to the Italian interpreter who accompanied me, that from two to three times as many persons occupied the room as the sign permits. One of these buildings, four stories high, is so old and rickety that it cannot stand alone, and has careened over against the building next to it. Everything is of wood, and if it was once on fire, with its narrow, obstructed halls and stairways, the swarm of tenants would burn like rats in a trap.

This is by no means an isolated case. When Rev. Mr. Barnett, of Whitechapel, London, was here a few days ago, one of the inspectors of the Board of Health took him to visit some of the tenement houses of South Boston and the North End. A *Boston Herald* reporter went with them, and I quote from his report of the trip: "The party first visited the tenement houses of South Boston, occupied for the most part by the fishermen and their families, and the poorer classes of the Irish population. The first one visited was the house known as the Slate block on First Street. Here was seen one of the best examples of the worst class of dwellings, and one in which legislation had accomplished but little. Here was a building where the law had not been complied with regarding whitewashing, and the walls were dirty and stained with smoke. Hardly a house was seen, in the whole course of the journey, where this simple law in the interest of health and sanitary condition of living had been observed. In many cases, it appeared as though it had not only been neglected this spring, but for many springs in the past. In driving from this section of the city to the North End, Mr. Barnett made the somewhat startling remark, 'We have nothing nearly so bad as this in Whitechapel.'"

Doesn't it seem a little strange to an outsider that the Board of Health keep on hand, as it were, block after block of tenement houses, where both landlords and tenants deliberately set the law at defiance, which they can show off at call? There could not be a greater folly than to put this question aside as a matter only interesting to those poor people themselves. The slavery of Uncle Tom and his woolly-

UNDER-GROUND TENEMENT WITH TWO BEDS.

headed children cursed the plantation house, in the end, as much as it did the cabin. We must look after these people and help them for the sake of others, if not on their own account. Dr. John S. Billings, in an address before the American Academy of Political and Social Science in February of this year, says: "When diphtheria prevails in a tenement house, many school children are endangered, and the most perfect plumbing in a house affords little protection against the entrance of this disease, if it is prevailing in the vicinity. Typhus and smallpox do not confine their ravages to the vicious and foul, after they have acquired malignancy amongst them. Mingled with those who might not be worth saving, is a much larger number of honest, industrious, and fairly intelligent and energetic poor people who live by days' wages, and are struggling against their surroundings to improve their condition, and especially to give their children a fairer chance in the race for life than they themselves have had. These last are the people whom it is worth while to help for their own sake. You will observe," says this cool-headed doctor, "that I am considering this matter entirely from the money point of view, without reference to religion or morals or altruism. The question, 'Am I my brother's keeper?' is far more important, I admit; but I confine myself to a lower plane — to the bread-and-butter aspects of municipal life. Great numbers of the incompetent, vicious, idle, deformed, or starved-brain class have been poured into this country by immigration during the last fifty years, and have filled our slums and tenement houses, our hospitals, asylums, almshouses, and jails to overflowing. They cannot escape the results of their physical organization, which, in its turn, is an inherited result of ancestral degeneration. For them we may 'hope the best, but hold the present, fatal daughter of the past.' Their death rates are from two to three times as great as those of the better class of population; one-fourth of their sickness is treated by charities, and one-third of those who die among them are buried at public expense. The districts in which they live require a larger proportion of the work of city officials, inspections, removal of nuisances, police, the courts, etc.; and, on the other hand, they contribute but little to municipal or other taxation. All this is well known; but we have not yet arrived at the stage of applying efficient and systematic prevention, which is perfectly possible, and are still pottering with the so-called remedies which are of little use. In these districts the deaths usually outnumber the births, so that if it were not for a continued stream of new recruits this population would diminish. How can accessions be prevented? One way is to get rid of and prevent additions to the kind of dwellings these people seek. Do you say that they must live somewhere, and that there must be such places for such people? I do not think so. It is not necessary that any city should allow the existence of any such houses within its limits; and if their destruction forces some persons into the almshouses, and drives others away, it will be the cheapest and best in the end."

There are scores, and I think I should be safe to say hundreds, of tenement houses within the city limits of Boston which are unfit to be inhabited, and where the landlords do not pretend to obey the laws of health required by the statutes, and yet the tenants are paying a sufficiently large rent to pay good interest on a clean, healthful tenement. Our modern science and our Christian civilization are alike challenged by this condition of things.

Yet, as you think of the horror of these Boston "cabins" and their miserable tenants, you will say, "They are at least free, they cannot be bought and sold like Uncle Tom." Alas! they are not free. True, no one can take them to an auction-block, but their bondage is none the less real. Into that fearfully neglected Italian tenement house which I have tried to describe in this discourse, the sweater had come, and women were making a fine class of knee pants for twenty cents a dozen pairs, which means forty cents a day in wages. These people find it impossible to save. The lower strata of wages in Boston, and in all our large cities, has reached the point where the people who depend on them labor simply to exist. One day's sickness in father or mother or child leaves a gap it takes weeks or months to bridge over again.

Sometimes a Southern Uncle Tom or Aunt Chloe had their son or daughter sold out of their arms, leaving them with broken hearts. But the white slaves of the tenement house

TWO O'CLOCK IN THE MORNING.

sound every deep of human agony. Think what it is to try to raise boys honest, when their playmates are thieves from the cradle! Think of the agony of a mother fighting the wolf of starvation day and night and finding, as, one Boston mother did only a few weeks ago, that the wolf of lust had devoured her one ewe lamb before she was yet thirteen years of age! Brothers, it is not yet time for the "abolitionist" to put aside his tocsin or his sword while so many of our brothers and sisters are living and sighing in their despair: —

> "Where home is a hovel, and dull we grovel,
>   Forgetting that the world is fair;
> Where no babe we cherish lest its soul perish,
>   Where our mirth is crime, our love a snare."

VIII

SOCIAL MICROBES IN BOSTON TENEMENT HOUSES, AND HOW TO DESTROY THEM

"Ring in the valiant man and free,
   The larger heart, the kindlier hand;
   Ring out the darkness of the land,
Ring in the Christ that is to be."
         ALFRED TENNYSON: *In Memoriam.*

VIII

SOCIAL MICROBES IN BOSTON TENEMENT HOUSES, AND HOW TO DESTROY THEM

THE greatest claim Job ever makes for himself is that in the days of his prosperity, when everybody knew him and was obsequious to him as a rich man, he was not only kind to the poor, but exhibited for them a genuine sympathy which was illustrated in his carefully searching out the causes of their troubles.

There is a good deal that passes for kindness and sympathy, in these days, that is nothing more than lazy good-nature. Ignorant or indifferent charity is often as mischievous in its results as the wicked greed of the skinflint and the miser. Sympathy, to be worth anything, must be incarnated, as in Job's case, so that it becomes feet to the lame and eyes to the blind. Frances Power Cobbe declares that the most Christ-like thing she ever heard from human lips, was from the "Good Earl" of Shaftesbury : —

> "'The friend of all the friendless 'neath the sun;
> Whose hand had wiped away a thousand tears ;
> Whose eloquent lips and clear, strong brain have done
> God's holy service through his fourscore years."

When he was speaking to her one day, in his study, of the wrongs of young girls, which he had just been investigating, the tears came to his eyes and his voice trembled. After a pause, he added, "When I feel how old I am, and know I must soon die, I hope it is not wrong, but I feel I cannot bear to go and leave the world with all the misery in it."

People who have no genuine sympathy for their fellows, oftentimes grow harder-hearted at a revelation of the miseries of the oppressed, which stirs nobler souls to their profoundest depths and awakens them to all manner of helpful benevolence. There is an old legend of St. Hilary Loricatus, who scourged himself so perpetually that his skin became like the hide of a rhinoceros. So, acquaintance with the sorrows and woes of the poor and unfortunate, acquired out of a morbid curiosity, or a hunger for that kind of emotion experienced by the reader of sensational novels, will result only in marring and hardening us.

Very different is the result of such knowledge when obtained through an earnest sympathy and a holy ambition to assuage the sorrows of the distressed. Shelley never wrote anything more beautiful, perhaps, than this: —

> "In sacred Athens, near the fane
> Of Wisdom, Pity's altar stood;
> Serve not the unknown God in vain,
> But pay that broken shrine again,
> Love for hate, and tears for blood."

I put this emphasis on the need of searching out the wrongs of the poor, because I am satisfied that one of the greatest factors in the present tenement-house situation is the ignorance and indifference of the people as to the condition of things in the slum tenement house. I am sure that nothing but good can come from an honest attempt to "let in the light of day upon the landlordism of the slums, as you have let it in upon Mormonism, and other hateful things that prefer darkness rather than light."

We need to bear in mind constantly, in considering this question, that society is a whole, and that an evil in one class of our citizenship cannot help but have its vicious influence, in a greater or less degree, upon every other portion of society. We must also remember that the bad tenement house is the birthplace and cradle, and to a large extent the schoolroom, of multitudes of boys and girls who are to exert their influence on every phase of our city life in the near future. Modern scientists have pursued the study of disease microbes with such diligence, that they claim to be able to recognize beyond mistake the germs of certain diseases. They find them in the atmosphere almost everywhere, and they prove that these microbes are real germs of disease, by their experiments with the lower animals.

The soil under our feet is full of these microorganisms. The smallest quantity of earth put in water reveals, through the microscope, besides the organic and mineral matter, a mass of beings more or less complex, moving more or less rapidly. A German author, Mr. Reimers, has calculated that every cubic centimetre of earth may contain several million germs.

EXTERIOR OF A NORTH END TENEMENT

Among these microbes some have not been studied, and the part they play in the economy of life is not known to us, while certain others have functions which have been well determined. Carbuncle, for instance, is one of the most terrible maladies which can attack cattle, and sometimes even men. Now-a-days, thanks to the labors of the scientists, this malady had become quite rare, and tends more and more to disappear. For a long time it has been known that carbuncle has been due to a particular microbe, but it was not known how it was propagated. M. Pasteur has demonstrated that this propagation was due, in part at least, to the longevity of the germs.

Thus it is, if you bury the dead body of an animal which has died of carbuncle, in a ditch five or six feet deep, and cover it with earth, the carbuncle bacteria will be found in the neighboring soil several years after the interment. We can understand, then, that cattle put to graze on this land, or fed by provender from it, may contract the disease. So when the cause of this malady was unknown, it is not to be wondered at that superstitious country people called these places "cursed fields."

There are social microbes no less potent and mischievous than those with which Pasteur deals. Some of those who are infected with the contagion are put away in pest-houses or in prisons; many more walk the streets, and spread their dangerous infection through the social, business, and home life of the people. My claim is that the bad tenement house in Boston, as everywhere else where people are herded together in crowded filthy quarters, where sanitary laws are neglected or defied either by landlords or tenants, or both, furnishes a breeding-place for the microbes of nearly every sin and vice that infest our modern society. The editor of the Portland *Oregonian*, commenting on General Booth's scheme for the rescue of the London poor, says: "Its most hopeful features are those which propose to provide the lowly with means to help themselves, in the building and maintenance of homes. Thousands of women belonging to the 'submerged tenth' need almost as much instruction in the simple acts of housewifely

WIDOW AND TWO CHILDREN IN UNDER-GROUND TENEMENT.

thrift and neatness, as the squaws belonging to the North American Indian tribes.

"Homes, in the civilized sense of the term, they have never had to keep, and their squalid abiding-places, overrun with wretched and quarrelsome half-clad children, and bare of the commonest comforts of life, have offered very unattractive fields for womanly originality and painstaking endeavor. A cheerful, quiet home, wherein the laborer is always sure of warmth and light and wholesome food, has in it a saving grace which all the creeds in Christendom cannot compass without its auxiliary aid."

The power of the liquor traffic, and all the other kindred vices that cluster about it, is constantly re-enforced by the social conditions of the neglected tenement house. Temptation enters as largely into drunkenness as into any other vice; and in the foul and fetid courts of the North End, the West End, South Boston, and the Cove, temptation to vice of every kind is ever present. The words of George R. Simms, in his earnest study of life in the homes of the London poor, apply with equal force to such sections in Boston: "The complete lack of home comforts, the necessity of dulling every finer sense in order to endure the surrounding horrors, the absence of anything to enter into competition with the light and glitter of the gin palace, and the cheapness of drink in comparison with food, all these contribute to make the poor easy victims to intemperance. Among the poor, the constant war with fate, the harassing conditions of daily life, and the apparent hopelessness of trying to improve their condition, do undoubtedly tend to make them 'drown their sorrows,' and rush for relief to the fiery waters of that Lethe which the publican dispenses at so much a glass. Ask any of the temperance workers in the viler districts, and they will tell you how they have watched hundreds of decent folk come into a bad neighborhood, and gradually sink under the degrading influences of their surroundings. There are few men who have worked to keep their brethren from the clutches of the drink fiend who would not gladly hail the advent of air, and light, and cleanliness, and the enforcement of sanitary laws, as the best weapons with which to do doughty deeds in their combats with intemperance among the poor."

One of the hardest things to deal with, in an attempt to arouse good people who are well-to-do and steadily prosperous to a serious study of the troubles of the poor, is to shake them out of the erroneous conviction that it is always the fault of the poor that they are in financial straits and compelled to resort to such places of dwelling. Put yourself in your brother's place, and listen to this true story of New England life enacted during the past year.

There lived, until a little over a year ago, in Western New York, a family which we will call Simmons, — far removed from the real name. The family consisted of the husband and wife, each about thirty-five years of age, and four children, — the eldest ten. Mr. Simmons was a confectioner by trade, but for some years had been travelling for a wholesale grocer's house in New York. He was a man of good address, and was fairly successful until, in some of the competitions of trade, the New York house determined to withdraw from that section, and he was thrown out of business. After casting about for several weeks in a vain attempt to get employment, he decided to bring his family with him to New England. They removed to Worcester, where for months he sought employment, but was unable to find anything except short jobs for a day or two at a time. Mrs. Simmons, who was an educated and refined woman, and a most worthy lady in every respect, did what she could to assist her husband; but as a fifth child was born to them in the autumn, she was so weakened by sickness and the care of her children, that she could do little besides looking after them. As the months passed, they were compelled to resort to the pawnshop — the bank of the unfortunate. First went their silverware, which was mostly wedding presents, an anguish to part with to people of their history and character. Then followed their best clothing, and some splendid books out of a well-selected library — for remember that these were educated, intelligent people, with all the instincts and tastes of good breeding. Finally, discouraged with Worcester, they removed, with what they had left, to Boston. Again for weary days, stretching into weeks, went on the disheartening search for work. Mr. Simmons says in those days the very iron entered into his soul. To see his refined, cultivated wife sick and wasting away, his children im-

THE BANK OF THE UNFORTUNATE.

properly clothed and hungry, and compelled, day by day, to return to the tenement house on the filthy street whither his condition had forced him, with a feeling of utter helplessness, he declares that nothing but the religious convictions of his youth, and the sense of the cowardice of the act, saved him from the death of the suicide.

During the winter they were compelled to sell their excellent cooking-range, which they had brought with them from New York, and procure a cheaper one. All the books that were left followed; then the bedsteads and other furniture went, until there was only one bedstead left, and that was rented through the day to a man who worked nights. Many days they had nothing to eat but bread or crackers — and often that was of a stale quality and a scant allowance. The eldest, a little boy, attended the Sunday-school of a Boston church; he has one of the truest, noblest, and most interesting faces I have ever seen. On missing him for a couple of Sundays, the superintendent of the school went in search of him, and for the first time knew of the condition of the family.

The Sunday-school superintendent found his little scholar lying in a dry-goods box, — for there was no bed in the daytime, — sick from lack of food and clothing. He made inquiries of the mother, and at last, with sobs and tears,

OUT OF WORK.

she told their story. Their necessities were relieved, and through the sympathetic interest of a number of Christian men the husband now has steady employment. Now, it is easy to say that he should have gone to the church, or the charities, with the story of his condition — and I think that is true; but, on the other hand, you can see that it was the very worthiness of the family, their very nobility, that made that course seem more bitter than starvation. Bear in mind that these people were not dissipated, that they were strictly moral and religious, and that both father and mother were of prepossessing appearance. This man did not drink, or smoke, or chew, and was intensely anxious to take care of his family; he was willing to do the humblest work, and preferred death to begging or dishonor.

Only a few weeks since, I called, with a brother minister, on a family of Maine people in a miserable tenement house in the North End. The husband and father had been sick and out of work for a good while. A short time before my visit, however, he had shipped on a coaster from Hyannis to Philadelphia. He had arranged for a little credit for his family to keep them from starving, until his expected return; but the winds had been contrary, and he was several days overdue. The wife and four children were in despair. They had had nothing since the morning of the day before, and then only bread and water, except a little broth which a neighbor, not much better off, brought in to one of the children — a beautiful little girl, sick with what would be "la grippe" on Beacon Hill, but is only "grip" down in the slums. The mother had a little babe, and was in such delicate health that it was impossible for her to go out to wash or scrub. Her two narrow little rooms were scrupulously neat and clean, as were her children; but the tears ran down her cheeks as, in answer to our questions, she confessed, as if she had been admitting a crime, poor soul, that they had had nothing to eat all day.

I give you these instances to show you how false is the idea that poverty and enforced residence in a miserable tenement house are a badge of sin or wrong-doing. But think of the agony of fathers and mothers, who love their children as well as you love yours, and have ambitions for them as holy and pure, who are compelled to see their loved ones deteriorating under their eyes, and through the contam-

A CHEAP LODGING-HOUSE.

ination of the poisonous moral atmosphere which they breathe, dropping slowly, but certainly, down to a level with the brutality which surrounds them.

Well, you ask, what is the remedy for all

this? My main purpose, in this series of discourses, was to place the facts of the situation before the people. But I have some plain, practical, common-sense suggestions to make. In the first place, we want an almost *infinitely* better system of inspection of tenement houses. Every tenement house in the city, having as many as eight families in it, ought to be inspected carefully, at least once a month — and once a week would be better — by an officer who holds his place under civil-service rules, entirely independent of politics, and who is held to a strict responsibility for the performance of his duties.

As to the tenement-house sweat-shop, I am convinced that a very simple law, which ought to be passed by the next legislature, requiring every manufacturer, of any kind, to file with the inspector of factories a list of the names and addresses of the people who work for him, would work wonders. It may be that there are some firms as low down as the one whose superintendent remarked the other day, when asked what the effect would be in their business if it were known that their goods were manufactured in filthy tenement houses: "It would make no difference at all; our customers would buy of us just the same, no matter where our garments were made." This firm, I am sure, would find itself mistaken, and, with a great many others, would break off its connection with the sweating-business if the law forced it to make that relation public.

Yet I am sure that nothing promises so much for reform as a revival of conscientious landlordism. The landlord is now, too often, as one well says, "an enormous wealthy estate, with heirs scattered here and there, who hire an agent, as their Southern brothers hired an overseer, irresponsible, unsympathetic, caring only to please his patrons, by showing a large balance of profit. And the poorer the tenement, the larger the balance. No repairs, no janitor, no supervision to pay for; accommodations so wretched that only the very wretched, who will expect to be crowded and miserable, will apply for it. O landlord! or 'estate!' too busy to collect your own rents, be not too indolent to require of your agent a strict account when he brings you twenty per cent instead of six! You would quickly bring him to book if he were suddenly to hand you six instead of twenty, but the time to question him is when it is twenty."

Mrs. Alice Wellington Rollins says in the *Forum*, speaking of New York: "Nothing is more astonishing, in investigating the slums, than the discovery of the enormous prices the poor are paying for the most wretched accommodations. One man boasts that he draws thirty-three per cent on his tenement investments." The same writer wisely says, farther: "The landlord is not to be a philanthropist, willing to sacrifice himself for the good of others; he is to be an intelligent capitalist, putting in his money purely as an investment, and philanthropic only to the degree of being satisfied with six per cent returns, of hiring a janitor to be on hand day and night, of being his own agent, or keeping a sharp lookout on the one he may have to employ, and of urging his wife to collect the rents. But individual landlordism need not necessarily be confined to individual persons. Individual corporations can become landlords. Why should not some of the insurance companies that complain of being unable to find suitable investments for their immense funds, take hold of the tenement question? A life-insurance company of Boston, complaining of the low rates of interest obtainable, announce that they never expect over five per cent, and find it difficult at times to get four.

"Half of the trouble is caused by the wilful cruelty, but half by the thoughtlessness, of the landlords. A wise writer has said recently: 'Often you don't need to say to a man, " *Why* do you do so?" If you can show him *what* he is doing, it is often enough to rouse him to reform.' I have faith enough in human nature to believe that if we could organize a procession of landlords and compel them to walk through the tenement districts, they would begin the reform themselves."

Let me relate to you a very interesting experiment that has indeed long since passed the era of experiment. In 1879 Mrs. Alice N. Lincoln and a young lady friend were so wrought upon by the filth and misery which they saw in certain tenement houses visited by them, in connection with the Associated Charities, that they determined to do something to better the condition of these poor people. They hired a large house on the corner of Chardon and Merrimac Streets. It contained twenty-seven tenements, and the rent agreed upon with the owner was one thousand dollars a year, though since the first year they have paid twelve hundred. The house had the worst possible reputation morally, and had been under the ban of the police for a long time.

It was, at the time they took it, half empty, because of the degraded character of the occupants. Its entries and corridors were blackened with smoke, and dingy and uninviting. The sinks were in dark corners, and were foul and disease-breeding. The stairways were innocent of water or broom, and throughout the entire house, from top to bottom, ceilings, walls, stairways — everything was dirty and neglected. It was surely not an attractive task to attempt to bring cleanliness and order out of such chaos, but these resolute young reformers deliberately set themselves to perform the seemingly impossible. The interior was painted, improved means of lighting and ventilating the sinks were ordered, and wood and coal closets arranged for each tenement on its own landing.

Previously the tenants had to keep their fuel in the cellar. The mouldy wall-paper was removed from the entries, and a fresh surface of plastering was put on. A few of the worst tenants had to be removed, but the majority, pleased with the new administration of things, were willing to accept its rules and remain. Tenants were soon found for every room; and this house, which had been regarded as very unhealthy, and had been a regular hive for fevers under the old *régime* of carelessness and greed, that did not care how dirty the tenants were so long as they paid their rent, under the new rule of cleanliness became so healthy that disease was almost unknown, and was, and is to this day, known by the tenants and the neighborhood generally as the "Good Luck House." The ladies collected their own rents, and kept everything well under their own supervision. A close account was kept of all receipts and expenditures, and at the end of the first year the balance of cash in hand was $111.67, or more than eleven per cent on the investment. The second year it was still more profitable, the net sum at the end of the year being $157.47. Mrs. Lincoln still carries on the administration of the "Good Luck House," and no queen was ever

THE "GOOD LUCK" TENEMENT HOUSE.

treated with more genuine respect than she is there. She is regarded as a most practical sort of patron saint to the institution. Yet there is no element of charity suggested in her dealings with her tenants. It is simply Christian justice. She seeks with great care to help them retain their self-respect, and treats them as fully her equal in personal responsibility. The rent is required to be paid regularly. One rigid rule enforced upon all tenants is cleanliness. She pays for the weekly scrubbing of the halls and stairways, but the tenants are required to sweep them every day, in turn. The sinks and drains are kept clean. All this has a marvellous effect on the home habits of the inmates; and I have seen as clean and tidy rooms in the "Good Luck" tenement house as I have seen anywhere, and that, too, on days when they were caught unawares, it not being the regular rent day, when they expect the landlady. All above six per cent has been put in the bank as an emergency fund, and, from time to time, the tenants have been permitted to share some unexpected pleasure from this. Once a splendid entertainment was given the tenants, in a public hall, with stereopticon views; at another time, it took a more material method of expression, and a good blanket, a pitcher and basin for each family, came out of this fund. In every way the tenants are made to know that their interests are in perfect harmony with those of the landlady. To encourage them to use more room, where they are able to pay for it, a discount is made on each additional room taken, and ten cents a week is deducted for payment in advance. A majority of them avail themselves of this privilege.

If he who makes a tree to grow where none grew before, is a public benefactor, surely she who has made it possible for many family-trees to grow and thrive, yielding their fragrance and their fruit in a pure home and social life, is a benefactress in the highest sense.

Let us encourage on every side the transformation of filthy, neglected tenements into "Good Luck" houses.

A little wise thoughtfulness may vastly improve the childhood of the slums. Boys' clubs and girls' clubs are steps in the right direction. They awaken an interest in innocent games, afford a glimpse of beautiful pictures, and give zest to the intellectual appetite for fresh, wholesome books. The "sand garden" is also a happy thought. Think of thousands of children reared in the narrowest, filthiest quarters, who have never had a chance to make even a mud-pie out in the pure air of heaven. It may seem a small thing to some, but it is a tragedy to me. When I remember my own happy childhood over in the Oregon woods, where I

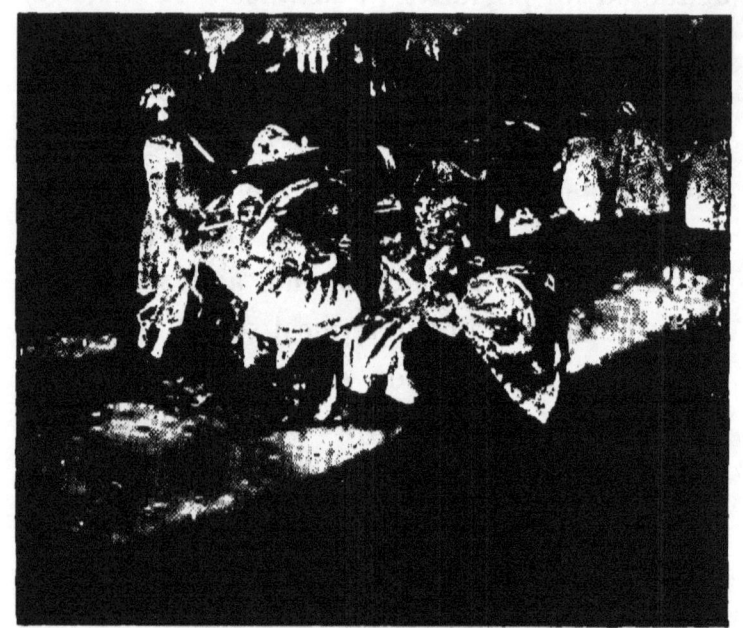

THE SAND GARDEN.

ran as free and untrammelled as a young colt in the pasture, and made mud-pies beside the brook that had its home in a great bubbling spring on the hillside, breathing the air fragrant with the perfume of wild lilies, while robins and bobolinks and meadow larks sported and sang without fear, on every side — when I contrast a childhood like that with the child-life in the Boston slums, I am heart-broken. There is nothing so sad as this "murder of the innocents" that is going on in all our great cities. Marianne Farningham sings their dirge: —

> "Such sights there are in the great sin-soiled city,
>   As might compel an angel into pity;
>   But none more sad in all the world of care,
>   Than a young child driven to black despair!"

Surely, trumpet blast never called men and women to a holier crusade than this rescue of the lost childhood of the slums.

IX

OLD WORLD TIDES IN BOSTON

"There is a poor blind Samson in this land,
    Shorn of his strength and bound in bonds of steel,
  Who may, in some grim revel, raise his hand,
    And shake the pillars of this Commonweal,
  Till the vast temple of our liberties
    A shapeless mass of wreck and rubbish lies."

    HENRY WADSWORTH LONGFELLOW: *The Warning.*

IX

OLD WORLD TIDES IN BOSTON

TRAVELLERS tell us that in some parts of the ocean, when the waves are still and the water is perfectly quiet, the curious eye may look down through the clear depths and see, rising out of the ocean's bed, the gnarled and broken trunks of forest trees. Once this ocean-bed was above the water-line, and these trees grew in the sunshine and stretched their branches upward to the blue sky of heaven. But, as the result of some strange convulsion of the earth, the coast-line has sunk down and down, until the incoming tide of the salt sea has swept over it, and schools of porpoises and fishes swim among the branches of old forest trees that in the former time were accustomed to the chatter of squirrels and songs of birds.

Any one studying the older and more historic sections of Boston will see many relics of a past civilization by which he will be impressed in very much the same way as is the sailor who looks on the remains of an ancient forest in the ocean's bed. Standing in the North End, in front of the "Copp's Hill Burying-ground," and looking up at the tower of Christ Church where the famous signal lanterns were hung, one can almost hear the old church appropriating the words of the poet: —

> "By time's highway — a milestone gray —
>   I watch the world march by;
> An endless stream of moving men
>   Rolls on beneath mine eye.
> Still, still they go; where, none can know;
>   And when one wave is gone,
> Another and another yet
>   Come ever surging on."

It seems strange indeed to go up and down some of these old historic streets, and yet never in the course of one's walk hear spoken the language of the country. In the course of my investigations during the past few months, I have found it impossible to do anything practical without an interpreter, sometimes in one language, and again in another. Often in entering an old rear tenement house, where filth and

CHRIST CHURCH TOWER.

misery held riot, I have been astonished at the splendidly carved ornaments over the doorways, and the still-to-be-traced carving on the balustrade. Once these old rear tenements were the abodes of Boston's wealthiest and most cultivated citizens; but the Old World tide has come in, and house after house, block after block, and street upon street, have been overwhelmed by the waves of people who speak other languages, and whose habits of life are more foreign than their speech.

I have no sympathy with those people who are crying out against all foreigners, yet it seems to me that no serious student of the signs of the times can take other than a sober view of the submerging tide of foreign immigration which has come into this country, of which the North End of Boston is a suggestive illustration. The consideration which causes the most sober thought among earnest men to-day, is the entirely different class of immigration coming to us now from that of former times. In the earlier days of American history it was the intelligent, self-reliant part of the European communities who dared the expense and hardship of the long sea voyage by a sailing-vessel, and faced the exigencies of the New World. The immigrants of those days were mostly farmers and skilled mechanics, who brought with them the habit and prestige of success. But under the new order of things, with the great steam ferries which make a passage to America only a brief holiday trip of a week, with reduced rates, and controlled by companies who scour every European city, by aid of their agents, to gather in their human cargoes from the poorest and most ignorant of all the labor classes, it becomes a very different question.

The motives that impel people to this country now, are very different from what they used to be. The San Francisco *Alta* well says: "The time was when the majority of foreign immigrants came because of an intelligent devotion to free government. Ninety-nine per cent of them were free from merely material motives. They were not urged by starvation, they did not come in the squalid steerage, they did not, on landing, feel compelled to invent servile occupations, before unknown in this country, merely to get the crusts and scraps that would keep them alive. Their motive was intellectual more than material. Their descendants are found in

ON THE CUNARDER.

every State, of good report, foremost among the fibres that make up American character.

Their blood may have been in the beginning English, Irish, Scotch, French, Italian, Spanish, German, Scandinavian, or Slav. No matter: they are now Americans, because the expatriation of their ancestors was real, and not unreal. Its motive was ethical, and not material. At present ninety-nine per cent of all immigrants come for material reasons only. Their decision to migrate to the United States is not for lack of liberty, but for lack of bread. The purpose is animal entirely. Every old emigrant from any country in Europe knows this to be so. The Italian who genuinely expatriated himself, who believed in Joseph Mazzini, and sought liberty for its own sake, finds no fraternity in the Italian immigration that has poured upon us since the suppression of the murder guilds of Sicily, and the decline of the industry of assassination in that country."

I think it is indeed one of the hopeful features of the situation that nearly all our adopted citizens, who are themselves thoroughly Americanized, share strongly in this view. Indeed, many of them seem to realize the danger more keenly than do the native-born citizens. I was

ON THE WAY TO THE RABBI.

very much interested, at the New England Chautauqua the other day, to hear Mr. John M. Langston, the colored orator of Virginia, read a letter from a leading Hebrew of Washington City, in which he reminded Mr. Langston that he had often pleaded the cause of the Negro, and appealed to him in turn to plead the cause of the Hebrew, by arousing public sentiment against the too rapid influx of Russian Jews.

The swift incoming of these Old World tides has very close relation to the wages of laboring people. Large numbers of the alien laborers who are coming now, are little better than "slaves of contractors, steamship lines, and the professional European jobbers in pauper labor. The large proportion of those engaged in our mines and on public works have been secured through these sources, either in direct defiance of our laws or by the evasion of the laws. They come in direct competition with the native-born and the worthy foreign immigrant, who comes here for the purpose of applying for citizenship and securing a home. They not only come into competition with every worthy class of laborers, but they are, for the most part, too ignorant to comprehend Ameri-

PASSING THE QUARANTINE DOCTOR.

can institutions, and have no broader idea of liberty than to insist that it includes license.

At every point of contact with our labor system, they debase it."

An illustration of this class of labor may be found in the fact that a year or two ago forty-seven alien miners employed in phosphate mines near Waterboro, S. C., were imprisoned because they refused to fulfil the contract under which they had been employed. Their story was that they had been met at Castle Garden by labor agents who induced them to sign a paper which they did not understand, but which proved to be a contract to work for one and two dollars a week in the phosphate mines, and board themselves. When they learned, on their first payday, of the trick which had been played upon them, they revolted. A few days in jail, however, induced them to return to work on the old terms.

The Chicago *America*, commenting on the incident, says this picture is a startling contrast to the prate of demagogues concerning the dignity of American labor. While they scheme to get the votes of intelligent workingmen, labor in many parts of this country is being enslaved by means of the hordes of foreigners who are imported in violation of law and right. Mr. Powderly tells, in the *North American Review*, of a visit which he paid to a mining-camp to investigate the condition of the men who were imported to take the places of American workmen who had demanded higher wages for labor done. These men lived in huge barracks. Their dining-room, smoking-room, sitting-room, kitchen, and bedchamber were one. There were five rows of bunks, three deep, each one thirty inches in width and seventy-eight inches long — the first bunk eighteen inches from the floor, the next, supported by rough hemlock posts, but two feet above it, and a third two feet above the second one. Each bunk was filled with straw, and covered with coarse coffee-sack material for bed-clothing. Two rows of hemlock boards, each one twenty feet in length by three feet in width, constituted the tables. The men came in from the mines while he was present, and, before washing face or hands, sat down to their supper of salt pork, meal, and water. One hundred and five men lived in a building one hundred and sixty feet in length by thirty feet in width. He found no one to answer him in the English tongue. When it was bedtime they lay down without divesting themselves of a single article of clothing; some of them took off their shoes, but the majority did not even do that. These men took the places of American workmen who were receiving from two dollars to two dollars and a half per day. The compensation allowed them was but seventy-five cents a day, and board. As a careful investigation proved that fifteen and three-eighths cents would provide the food furnished each man, the outlay was but ninety and three-eighths cents a day. It is getting to be quite a common custom on railroads and in mines and other places where this class of laborers are employed, to attach to the waistband of each man a leather strap fastened to a large brass check, similar to a baggage check. Every check bears a number, and the man who carries it, or to whom it is fastened, is known by the number on his check. Mr. Powderly grimly comments: "Fancy the future of the American laborer, whose name is forgotten, and whose only means of identification rests with a brass check, which may be substituted for another while he sleeps." If this is not white slavery, what is it?

These Old World tides have also close relation to the health of our cities. Large numbers of these people have been accustomed to live in crowded quarters, on insufficient food, and without any regard for cleanliness, in their native country. They come here, bringing all their filthy habits, bred in them sometimes for generations. I have no doubt that some of my critics tell the truth when they say that the squalid tenements occupied by the Russian Jews and Italians in Boston are better than the homes whence they came. So far as these foreigners themselves are concerned, even these wretched conditions are perhaps an upward step in evolution. But if we are going to have Naples in Boston, we must expect to have Neapolitan cholera epidemics as well.

These Old World tides have also a very close relation to the morals of our people. An overwhelming majority of all the criminals who figure in our police courts, and are supported in our jails and penitentiaries, were born abroad. This is very easy to understand when one investigates a little the methods used to encourage emigration to this country. The in-

SURGICAL THEOLOGY.

vestigation made by the Ford Congressional committee revealed the enormous extent to which steamship companies are drumming Europe for human freight, to be dumped on our shores. "To these unscrupulous 'fishers of men' everything that walks or crawls is acceptable. Quantity, not quality, is the desideratum. The worse the specimen, the more effective, usually, is the emigration prize offered, and the less the opposition interposed by government officials. In a word, a drag-net has been thrown over nearly the entire European continent, with the result of having recently collected for shipment to this country a class of humanity, which, wherever it may be, is a menace to good order and a tax upon the police and charity departments of the country."

One who speaks with the highest authority on questions of political economy puts the immigration problem in a strong light when he says: "We are now draining off great stagnant pools of population which no current of intellectual or moral activity has stirred for ages. Thousands and hundreds of thousands of those who represent the very lowest stage of degradation to which human beings can be reduced by hopelessness, hunger, squalor, and superstition, are found among the new citizens whom the last decade has brought into the Republic." It is known beyond doubt that prisoners' aid societies in various European countries have been steadily shipping convicts to the United States. Neither has it been an uncommon thing for criminals to be let off by the courts, on condition of their emigrating to America. It is folly for us to expect to take this great criminal class, who were born to crime in the purlieus of European cities, who have been thieves from their cradles, and who come to us fresh from jails and prisons, and change them into useful citizens. They will not only continue to be criminals themselves, but they will spread their vile and wicked contagion wherever they go. There is not a single cause of reform or progress in this country that is not constantly discouraged and postponed by these Old World tides of ignorance and vice.

There can be no doubt that there is a rising tide of public sentiment in this country in favor of a careful and wise examination of every emigrant who offers himself as a candidate for

American citizenship in the future. I think, in view of the fact that we are getting a very large and increasing proportion of our immigration from Southern Europe, which is the most

BUILDING USED BY THE BRITISH AS A HOSPITAL.

illiterate portion of the Old World — in Southern Italy, for instance, seventy-nine out of every one hundred are illiterate — there ought to be an educational test. There is certainly no wisdom in our adding hundreds of thousands a year to the number of illiterates already here, who are unable to read the Declaration of Independence, and have not the faintest conception of the principles of our Constitution. The examination of emigrants ought to be on the other side of the water. We have had many recent illustrations in Boston of the manifest hardships experienced under the present arrangement. Every person intending to emigrate to America ought to be required to give notice of that desire through the nearest American Consul, and furnish a clean bill of health, both moral and physical; and no one should be permitted to sail without a certificate of such investigation and satisfactory finding. This would not shut out any one who would be of value to American institutions, but it would require European countries to care for the criminals and paupers which their own social system has bred.

But what shall we do with these multitudes of foreigners who are already living in our midst? In the first place, we must cease to regard them as foreigners or aliens, and set to work with a definite purpose to Americanize them as quickly as possible. We must not, for a moment, be satisfied to let them herd together in the filth and squalor to which they may have been accustomed at home. We cannot afford to hand them over to the greedy tyranny of the sweater. Nothing will help us more than the abolition of the neglected tenement house, and the provision for a healthier, cleaner shelter for the people.

Some of our public-spirited men of wealth cannot do better than to look in this direction as a field in which to make their mark upon the uplift of their race and their time. There is a far greater demand for this class of benevolent investments than there is for added colleges or universities. If some of the vile and unhealthy tenements that have been described recently, not only by myself but by the reporters and the daily press, could be replaced by such buildings as the Victoria Square building in Liverpool, it would be a great public benefaction. On the former site of Victoria Square were miserable tenement houses. To-day a magnificent structure stands there, built around a hollow square, the larger portion of which is given up for a healthful play-ground for the children. "The

VICTORIA SQUARE.

halls and stairways of the building are broad, light, and airy; the ventilation and sanitary arrangements, perfect. The apartments are divided into one, two, and three rooms each. No room is smaller than thirteen by eight feet six inches; most of them are twelve by thirteen feet four inches.

"All the ceilings are nine feet high. A superintendent looks after the building. The tenants are expected to be orderly, and keep their apartments clean. The roomy character of halls and chambers may be inferred from the fact that there are only two hundred and seventy-five apartments in the entire building. The returns on the total expenditure on the building, which was three hundred and thirty-eight thousand eight hundred dollars, it is estimated will be at least four and a half per cent." The rents will seem miraculous to those of you who have been following the prices given in this series of discourses. In this beautiful Victoria Square dwelling, with its large, shrub-encircled play-ground for children attached, light, airy, three-room tenements are furnished for one dollar and forty-four cents per week. For those containing two large rooms one dollar and eight cents a week is charged; while the one-room quarters are let at fifty-four cents a week.

Who among our rich men will lead off in some grand crusade of this sort? Another thing we want to do to Americanize these people, is to furnish them employment under conditions consistent with health, intelligence, and morality. Instead of the crowded sweat-shop, the moral atmosphere of which is as filthy as the physical, we must have factories conducted in the spirit of Christian civilization.

Let me tell you of a vision I had the other day as I sat meditating and dreaming in my study chair. I dreamed I was walking down the streets of an American city when I saw a large brick building which I might have thought was a factory except that there were white curtains at every window in the house. As I neared the door, I asked a passer-by what it was, and he astonished me by saying, "This is the great Christian factory." Being a little anxious to see what life in a really Christian factory would be like, I went in on a tour of investigation. There were several hundred employés in the factory, most of whom were young women. To my astonishment, I found bath-tubs in this factory, with an abundance of hot and cold water, linen towels, and toilet soap. Did one ever hear of such luxuries in a factory of any sort? In the girls' bath-room there were rugs under foot, the finishing was done in oak, the trimmings were nickel-plated, the sanitary arrangements were perfect, and everything was as bright and clean as it was possible to make it. Each employé was allowed thirty minutes for a bath, and if one was so fastidious as to need three-quarters of an hour, no comments were made. The structure was commodious and convenient, substantially built, and heated, lighted, and ventilated throughout according to the most improved system. Even the cellar was attractive in its completeness, from the steam-engine that operated the machinery of the building, to the culinary department where those who desired could purchase a noon-day lunch at actual cost of material. The cook in charge of the kitchen devoted her entire time to the work. Every day, tea, with milk and sugar, was supplied by the firm free of charge; oaten meal was furnished three days in the week at the same rate. Delicious soup was served at three cents a bowl. The entire floor was carefully cemented; it was light, warm, and clean, and there were tables and benches for those who lunched in the building. An hour was allowed at noon, and while all were expected to be on hand promptly at one o'clock, the girls living at a distance from the factory were thoughtfully permitted to leave a few minutes before twelve o'clock.

On the main floor goods were stored in the centre of the room, the remaining space being reserved for the pleasure and convenience of the employés. At one end of this spacious floor there was an improvised music-room, with a piano and window garden, where the girls could sing and sun themselves every noon. Opposite was an enclosed sanctum, divided into a reading and reception-room. Bright, soft rugs were scattered about. The reading-table

was as well stocked with current literature as a club man's library table. The papers and periodicals were reserved for the exclusive use of the girls. An open fireplace was one of the attractive features of the reception-room, and there was a mantel-mirror, too — that means of grace so dear to the gentler sex.

The two upper floors contained the worktables and machines. On entering these workrooms one was struck by the neatness of the place. Everything seemed to have a white lining. The atmosphere was not only clean, but fresh and sweet. There were no rags, no dust, no fluff, no smell of dripping grease from overhanging machinery. A special staff of men was constantly employed to look after the premises, and their vigilance was such as to anticipate the wear and tear. The abundance of light and sunshine would astonish and delight not only business people, but school commissioners as well. Each work-shop was the size of an entire floor, so that light was admitted from four sides of the building, the windows almost adjoining one another. The white curtains, which softened the light, gave the place a homelike appearance which was very pleasing. Another charm was the love of flowers. There were potted plants on every floor, and they were as green and lovely as if nourished by a practical florist. On making some inquiries, I found that Friday was pay-day, and that indirectly much good resulted from this thoughtful system. Not only did it give the hundreds of families the benefit of the early Saturday markets, but in a great measure did away with the credit-books, and, best of all, was instrumental in keeping the girls off the street Saturday night. No charges were imposed upon the operators. They did not have to buy thread, pay machine-rent, or replace broken needles. If an attachment was displaced, it was restored by the firm, and even the girls' scissors were kept sharpened at the expense of the employer. Hot and cold water, mirrors, towels, and soap were among the conveniences. Posted over the stationary wash basins was this request: "Please help with your forethought to keep things clean and nice. Any attention will oblige." This was signed by the firm. The work was so systematized, and the training so thorough, that the tyrannical forewoman and domineering foreman had no place in the establishment. The manager was the only person to whom the hands were accountable. Adjoining the factory was a pretty garden containing a pear-orchard, with arbors and seats, where the girls lunched in fine weather. Women as a class show the effects of good keeping, and these workers were not an exception. There were a great many pretty faces among them, and not one that betrayed "boss-fright" or time-terror. As a class they looked more like

normal college students than factory hands. Compared with overworked, nerve-strained, anxious-faced girls in the sweat-shops, and indeed in most shops and factories, these trim, tidy-looking, cheerful and contented women seemed to me the very *noblesse* of the industrial world.

Ah! you may say, that is only an idle and visionary dream; and no doubt my critic of a few weeks ago, who thought I belonged to the most dangerous class in the community when I was describing the misery of the " white slaves of the Boston sweaters," would be ready to say that I am engaged in a scarcely less dangerous task in putting such ideal and impossible dreams into the heads of working-girls. But, dear sceptical friend, what I have been telling you is not a dream at all, but a heavenly reality that is going on in this modern work-a-day world, in the city of Newark, N. J., and I have merely been summarizing for you the report of Nell Nelson in the New York *World*, giving an account of the Christian experiment of Ferris Brothers' factory for the making of corset waists.

I was at this point in my discourse on Thursday at half-past one o'clock, when I said to myself, " Isn't it a little hazardous to take all this for fact, even on the authority of a newspaper reporter? Will not a great many of your audience say it is only a pleasing fancy of a reporter's imagination?" So at three o'clock I was on the train for New York, and at eleven that evening I was in bed in a hotel in Newark.

Friday morning, at half-past seven, I was going through Ferris Brothers' factory. It is with great pleasure that I tell you that, on returning, I did not have to strike out a single word I had written. On every side were evidences of thoughtfulness; for instance, a large portion of the girls employed live in a section of the city to the rear of the factory. In order to save the extra walk of a block or two, three hundred additional keys have been made to the orchard gate, so that they can come and go that way. A large number of umbrellas are kept in the office. If a girl is caught at the factory in an unexpected shower, she finds an umbrella waiting to be loaned in just such an emergency.

With the manager I went through the culinary department. They make ice-cream now every day, and sell large plates to the girls for three cents. A careful account is kept of the cost, and the manager said he thought he should be able to reduce the cream to two cents a plate.

I looked through the reading-room and over the carefully selected lists of papers. The manager said that among the girls were some excellent musicians, and others with good literary abilities, and told me, I thought with a pardonable degree of pride, that a few months since, when some desirable positions in the Newark Public Library were open to competition, the two young ladies from the Ferris Brothers' factory who were successful, scored ninety-five points out of a possible hundred in their literary examination. No employé works more than nine and one-quarter hours a day, and Saturday afternoon is free. The average wages, including beginners and help girls, is seven dollars a week, and a good worker makes twelve dollars.

You may say that many of these things that I have mentioned are insignificant and only trifles, but, after all, it is such things as these that in a large degree make or unmake our human lives; and a human life is no trifle.

But lest some hard-headed business man shall shake his head and say, "The fools will bankrupt themselves," I must add, that aside from the beauty and grace of this thoughtful business philanthropy, the enterprise has been entirely satisfactory from a commercial standpoint, the firm agreeing that not only have their employés done more, but better, work than ever before. One of the firm assured me that, while there were, of course, many discouraging things and occasionally an employé who showed little appreciation, on the whole there had been a steady improvement during their three years' experience in this factory, and under no circumstances would they be willing to go back to the old factory *régime*.

To contrast a factory like this with some of the sweat-shops I have visited, is like contrasting heaven with hell. There may be, and I doubt not are, many other factories where the same Christian thoughtfulness is exercised in the treatment of employés, as here. Upon all such may the benediction of Heaven rest! May their numbers be multiplied!

The Church, too — I mean the great Catholic Church, formed of all the branches of our Christianity "who love the Lord Jesus Christ in sincerity" — must open its arms with a heartier tone of welcome and brotherhood to the tried and disheartened working-people. Nothing in recent art has stirred me so deeply as a dim copy of Hacker's "Christ and the Magdalene," reproduced by Mr. Stead in the *Review of Reviews*. The Christ is standing with coarse clothing and toil-worn hands by the work-bench in the carpenter-shop at Nazareth. The shavings are heaped in piles around him on the otherwise bare floor, while kneeling at his feet in penitence and trust is the Magdalene. Brothers, it is this carpenter Christ, as Frances Willard aptly puts it, " the Monday Christ," for whom the toil-worn world hungers, and will welcome when it sees Him manifested in us, in the shop, the factory, and the counting-room, as well as in the church.

Zoe Dana Underhill sings, in *Harper's Magazine*, a song the modern Church needs to learn, until its great heart shall throb with its spirit.

"The Master called to His reapers,
'Make scythe and sickle keen,
And bring me the grain from the uplands,
And the grass from the meadows green,

And from off the mist-clad marshes,
   Where the salt waves fret and foam,
Ye shall gather the rustling sedges,
   To furnish the harvest-home.'

Then the laborers cried, 'O Master,
   We will bring Thee the yellow grain
That waves on the windy hillside,
   And the tender grass from the plain;

But that which springs on the marshes
   Is dry and harsh and thin,
Unlike the sweet field-grasses,
   So we will not gather it in.'

But the Master said, 'O foolish!
   For many a weary day,
Through storm and drought, ye have labored
   For the grain and the fragrant hay.
The generous earth is fruitful,
   And breezes of summer blow
Where these, in the sun and the dews of heaven,
   Have ripened soft and slow.

' But out on the wide, bleak marshland
   Hath never a plough been set,
And with rapine and rage of hungry waves
   The shivering soil is wet.
There flower the pale green sedges,
   And the tides that ebb and flow,
And the biting breath of the sea-wind
   Are the only care they know.

' They have drunken of bitter waters,
   Their food hath been sharp sea-sand;
And yet they have yielded a harvest
   Unto the Master's hand.
So shall ye all, O reapers,
   Honor them now the more,
And garner in gladness, with songs of praise,
   The grass from the desolate shore.' "

X

OUR BROTHERS AND SISTERS, THE BOSTON PAUPERS

"And Sir Launfal said, 'I behold in thee,
An image of Him who died on the tree;
. . . . . .
Mild Mary's Son, acknowledge me;
Behold, through Him, I give to thee!"
JAMES RUSSELL LOWELL : *Sir Launfal.*

X

OUR BROTHERS AND SISTERS, THE BOSTON PAUPERS

"Now there was a certain rich man and he was clothed in purple and fine linen, faring sumptuously every day: and a certain beggar named Lazarus was laid at his gate full of sores."

"Inasmuch as ye did it unto one of these my brethren, even these least, ye did it unto Me."

THESE two views of poverty ever stand over against each other. They are the same to-day as when so graphically described by Jesus of Nazareth. The one looks on poverty with contempt; it is the view of selfishness. The other looks upon it with sympathetic brotherhood; the view of humanity at its highest attainment, or from the standpoint of Jesus Christ. Both these scriptures, however, agree in teaching us the solemnity of our relation to our neighbors who are in trouble or poverty. Mrs. Catherwood, in her story of "The Lady of Fort St. John," in the August *Atlantic Monthly* — a tale of the early French settlements in this country, illustrates one of the old superstitions by a weird tale of an old Hollander who had married a very young wife who, when he came to die, was still only a girl; and the cunning old Dutchman endeavored to maintain his supremacy over her after his death by grimly providing in his will that his right hand should be severed from his body, and, preserved by some rare chemical process, should always remain in the possession of his widow as her most sacred treasure; for if she lost or destroyed it, or failed to look on it once a month, nameless and weird calamities, foreseen by the dying man, must light not only on her, but on those who loved her best. And so, long after he was in his grave, that horrible memento of the past held this poor woman in the clasp of its skeleton fingers, and guided her course across the oceans, and into distant lands. This was the grip of a superstition only; but there is a real grip of the "dead hand," of which this ghostly story is only a faint intimation — the grip of yesterday on to-day — of to-day on to-morrow — the grip of my duty toward my neighbor that cannot be shaken off, which even death itself does not loosen.

There is, perhaps, no keener test of the standing of a person or a city in the scale of civilization, than their treatment of the sick or helpless poor dependent upon them. Dives, the barbarian, whether in Jerusalem two thousand years ago, or in Boston to-day, lets the poor lie at his gate in indifference, at the mercy of every scavenger that may prey upon them. The "Good Samaritan," whether on the road to Jericho, or at Rainsford Island, stops with sympathetic eye, a helpful hand, and open purse to share his best with the victim of misfortune or wrong.

We come this morning to examine into the attitude of Boston toward her paupers who are cared for in the two institutions at Long Island and Rainsford Island. I have made repeated visits to these islands, and approach this discussion only after many weeks of reflection, and a careful sifting of the information received. I have hesitated about treating the subject at all, because a criticism of a public institution is supposed by so many people to mean a personal accusation or attack upon the parties in charge of it. I wish to say, in the beginning, that so far as I have been able to see, the officers immediately in charge of these institutions are kind-hearted and humane, and are endeavoring to do the best they can, with the means at their disposal. After saying that, I propose, without any regard as to whom it may please or displease, to point out candidly what seems to me inexcusable thoughtlessness and grievous errors in the treatment of the paupers in these institutions.

The largest and best building is on Long Island. Here the men are kept. There are about three hundred on the average, but this is increased to between four and five hundred in the winter. And right here is a wrong that ought to be righted.

The excuse for careless and indifferent treatment of the really deserving pauper men who are on Long Island is that every winter the place is crowded with "bummers" who come to Long Island in the winter for free quarters, and as soon as the weather is fine for out-door tramping in the summer, they go away to escape work in the institution, coming back again in cold weather. It would certainly be very easy to devise a law to make this impossible. No able-bodied person who is able to

TRAMPS.

work, ought under any circumstances to be sent to the almshouse. People who are able to work and support themselves, and do not do so under their own direction, ought to be sent to the work-house, and compelled to do so under the direction of a proper officer. This would take away from Long Island a lot of drunken tramps who congregate there in the winter. The same remark applies to women. The intemperate and vicious woman ought not to be sent to the almshouse; it should be sacredly kept as "a refuge and a home where the respectable poor, the sick, and the old — those who have outlived their children, or have broken down in the race of life — may find shelter and care." But the honest cases ought not, and need not, suffer in order to punish these frauds. At Long Island, on one of my visits, there were ninety-two men on the sick-roll, and only one nurse, and he not a trained nurse. I am also satisfied that the food is insufficient either for sick or well. A reporter of the Boston *Post* managed to interrogate an old man who was able to sit up by the side of his little cot. In answer to a question, this sick old man said they did not get any milk; and yet there is a large farm attached to the institution, and there is no excuse for not having plenty of milk provided at very little expense for these infirm old people. The old man said they had meat three times a week —

remember that means three meals out of twenty-one; and when asked by the reporter, "What kind of meat?" he answered pathetically, "It wouldn't do any good for me to tell you, sir, but it's mighty poor stuff." Permit me to quote in full a little article in the Boston *Herald* of a few weeks since, under the title, "Some Harbor Policemen Overpowered by Long Island Hospitality:" —

"There is a little joke which is causing considerable merriment at the Harbor police station at the present time, and the key to it is contained in the words, 'Long Island hospitality.' A few days ago the police-boat 'Protector' was ordered to take to Long Island a party of surveyors, who were to lay out grounds for the proposed new hospital.

"The work of the boat's passengers occupied an unexpectedly long time, and as no provision had been made for dinner, the party invoked the hospitality of the almshouse on the island. The surveyors and officers of the boat were assigned to one part of the institution, while the crew were invited into the large dining-hall, usually occupied by the inmates. It is this last-named party which is bearing the brunt of the joke. The feast of which they were invited to partake consisted of a lot of potatoes with their jackets on, without the formality of a platter, a plate of what the boys termed 'soup-meat,' a soup-dish minus the soup, knives and forks, and empty mugs. Grace was omitted; the men spent the time in gazing first at the 'feast,' and then at each other. A common thought seemed to occupy the minds of all, for without a word they simultaneously arose from the table and left the room.

"They waited at the boat until the surveyors' work had been completed, and then came back to Boston. It was then time to make the regular afternoon trip, and with empty stomachs they started out again and finished the day. It was the intention of the victims to keep the matter 'shady;' but the joke leaked out, as such things will, and it is worse than shaking a red rag at a bull to say 'Long Island hospitality' to certain blue-coats who labor on the water." And yet they were there at one of the three lucky meals out of twenty-one, when there was "soup-meat."

Among the men in this institution was pointed out to me a marble-cutter, who was a thoroughly respectable, self-supporting workman. He was hurt while at work by the falling of a stone, and so disabled by an injury of the spine that he was unable to continue employment. As soon as sickness had used up what money he had, having no relatives who could help him, there was nothing left for him but to come here. One of the officers spoke of him in the highest terms, and told me how, without direction from any one else, he sought by many daily circuits of the building to strengthen his spine. I was assured by the same officer that many others who were inmates were there purely through misfortune which was from no fault of their own, but from such accidents as are likely to happen to any honest laboring-man. Now I maintain that such men ought to be treated with a decent regard for their self-respect, and given a comfortable home. It is an outrage that this marble-cutter, and others like him, are fed more shabbily than if they had been convicted of a crime.

In addition to the men on Long Island, there

is one ward in the hospital used for women. There were fifty-two sick women crowded into this ward at the time of my visit. There was only one nurse, an excellent woman, but with no special education for her duties. The night helper is a woman who is hired for fifty cents a day. For this ward of fifty-two sick women there was no bath-room at all. The nurse's own room was situated at the other end of the building from her ward, and she had to go across the men's ward to get to her patients at night, if she went. There was no place for insane or refractory patients, or for the dying, except in the general ward. Sometimes their cries and groans are very distressing to the other patients. In a recent case of death from mania, the whole ward was disturbed for several nights.

Most of the women are kept at Rainsford Island, and there are many more reasons for criticism there than on Long Island. The only hospital there is an old smallpox hospital, more than three-score years old. This is crowded beyond all thought of the requirements of sanitary science. Think of a room for confinement cases only seven feet wide and less than twelve feet long. In the annual report of Public Institutions for 1889 we find the following statement by the then resident physician: "It is remarkable that a building which was a smallpox hospital fifty-seven years ago, and which since then has undergone no material improvement, should up to the present time be the only hospital connected with our pauper institutions." The doctor might have added that this building was abandoned a quarter of a century ago by the State, as unfit for sick persons. It is certainly no extravagance to say that these arrangements for the care of the sick on Rainsford Island are more than half a century behind the times. The only thing modern I saw was the keen-eyed physician.

There is about the entire institution a lack of careful thoughtfulness for the comfort of the inmates, that is exceedingly painful to a thoughtful observer. For example, the island is very beautifully situated, and there are many fine trees in the shade of which, with comfortable arrangements, it would be a most healthful and delightful experience for hundreds of these infirm and aged women to sit on summer days; but, although I searched carefully throughout the grounds, I found only two benches under the trees anywhere, and a half-dozen more, perhaps, around on the sea-front, and not one of them with a back to it. Think of arranging for the comfort of your own grandmother, eighty years old, in that way!

The food here, too, is insufficient. For instance, the matron told me that only those who worked were allowed butter on their bread. These old women are set down to bread and tea for one meal, and bread and soup for another; they, too, have a little meat of some kind three times a week, and potatoes at dinner. Again I repeat that, with the large farm attached to Long Island, there is no reason why these old women, as well as the old men, should not have an abundant quantity and an appetizing variety of vegetables, as well as plenty of nourishing milk. And I maintain that it is a shame and disgrace that the Boston which less than five years ago could spend more than twenty thousand dollars in feasting and wining a Hawaiian woman who came to visit us, expending four thousand dollars for flowers alone, cannot afford to furnish a little butter to spread on the bread of the helpless old women on Rainsford Island, even if they are unable to work. Think of the stolid indifference, or thoughtlessness — to hunt for charitable words — of an institution having several hundreds of people to care for, and yet making no difference in its hospital diet. No matter what the disease, it is to eat up to the cast-iron programme, or starve. Who that has been ill or has watched anxiously with their own dear ones, but has noticed the capriciousness of a sick person's appetite, the longing for little delicacies, for just a taste of some rare and unusual dish or drink? Such things are not expensive; they only mean that somebody shall invest a little genuine sympathy and thoughtfulness in the matter. Throughout this entire institution, hospital and all, having over four hundred women, there is not a single trained nurse! In this day of enlightenment it ought to be a crime for any hospital to be carried on without trained nurses. There is no night watchman on the whole island, and, after eight o'clock in the evening, nobody who is responsible at all. In the main institution on Rainsford Island the attic is crowded with beds to such an extent as to make a healthful atmosphere impossible.

You must remember that many people here are paupers through no fault of their own. Many of them are victims of incurable disease; and, as against such cases the Boston hospitals are closed, the almshouse is for them the only open door. Public sentiment must be aroused to demand, with Florence Nightingale, that " work-house sick shall not be work-house inmates, but they shall be poor sick, cared for as sick who are to be cured if possible, and treated as becomes a Christian country if they cannot be cured." We people who are followers of Him who confessed, " The foxes have holes, the birds of the air have nests, but the Son of man hath not where to lay His head," cannot afford to treat people who are, through misfortune, in the same condition to-day as though they were some species of criminal, rather than as the hostages of our Christ. Perhaps you say these people are not appreciative, are not refined, do not have fine feelings — how do you know that?

That is doubtless true about some of them, but about many of them nothing could be more false. People do not lose their powers of appreciation when they lose their money, and I doubt not that these people would average, in the essential characteristics of manly and womanly character, with the same number of people of the same age you could gather from the homes along your street. Last Christmas some kind-hearted women went down to Rainsford with some gifts for the sick poor. One of them, writing about their reception, says: "It was very touching to see the happiness our little gifts conferred. The first was a poor old woman, more than eighty, nearly blind from cataracts over her eyes. She is called 'Welsh Ann' because she is from Wales. My friend told her I had been in Wales. She seemed so glad to shake hands with one who had been in her own country, and her voice choked with tears as she thanked me and took my gift. But she brushed the tears away from her poor sightless eyes while my friend repeated to her the Twenty-third Psalm, and then at her request knelt and prayed. The apron which I gave her has quite a history. A girl who earns her own living, hearing I was making these aprons, sent me this one which she bought. It was worked across the bottom, and I thought, as poor Ann rubbed her hands over the work she could not see, but only touch, how cheered the young lady would be when she heard of the joy her gift gave. I was asked to give one pretty apron to another Ann — one they called 'Greenland Ann,' because she is so very fond of hearing them sing 'From Greenland's icy mountains.'" And surely that spirit of the Christ, which is warm enough to impel men to dare the frost of "Greenland's icy mountains" in order to comfort with His blessed Gospel their Esquimau brother, ought to prompt us to deal thoughtfully and tenderly with the dear old soul that likes to hear Him sung about on Rainsford Island.

I shall never forget the impression made upon me by Mark Guy Pearse, one of the greatest of the English preachers, in his story of how he was ordained a preacher. He said: "It was no bishop or presbytery that consecrated me, but a saintly Cornish woman, whom we children called old Rosie, and who was, indeed, my right reverend mother in God.

"So far as I can recollect, it was always sunshiny when we visited old Rosie, though of course it must have rained sometimes. She had a single room in a tiny little cottage squeezed behind the rest. A narrow strip led to the door, and there was no room for any window in front, except the one right above the door, peering out from under the heavy thatch. There is no one to answer if we knock, so we push our fingers through the door and lift the wooden latch. My father, who goes with us almost every Sunday, has to stoop his head in climbing the narrow stair, and of course the little lad of six and his sisters stoop their heads too; there are four of the girls and one of me. Rosie welcomes us with her beaming smile. She is sitting up in bed, as she has done for eleven long years. She is a hundred and five years old, and her hair is snowy white, yet there is not a wrinkle on her brow, and her cheeks have the rosy brightness from which she gets the familiar name. All her relations are gone, and she is now a pauper with only two or three shillings a week from the parish.

"We might call her poor and lonely and bedridden, yet she is brimful of happiness. The Bible is constantly at her hand, and she is generally thanking God for all His mercies. She has lived in the light and love of the Saviour since she was eleven years old; and she has gone so long and so far in the good way, that now it is as if she were sitting just outside the golden gates, crowned with radiant beauty and clothed with white raiment, waiting until her Lord shall bid her enter.

"At dear old Rosie's bed we used to have a little service; first a chapter read from the Bible, then a hymn — 'Rock of Ages' was her favorite, sung to 'Rousseau's Dream.' When the prayer was over, old Rosie would lay her thin hand on the little lad's curly head, and say as she turned her face upward, 'O Lord, bless the little lad! Bless him and make him a preacher.' I didn't like that prayer of hers, and I used to say to myself, 'I will never be a preacher; I will be a doctor, and gallop about the country visiting people.' But one Sunday, after the service and her little prayer, she said 'good-by' to us all. 'You won't see me any more; so it must be good-by for a long time now, until we meet at home.' We wondered what she meant. Two days after, she was carried home by God's angels from her lonely room. My little heart was like to break at the thought of never seeing her again; and I went out by myself to the garden and prayed, 'Please God, I don't care so much, after all, if I become a preacher, if it will make dear Rosie any happier.'"

It would be better for us that a millstone were hanged about our necks, and we were cast into the depths of the sea, than that we should be thoughtless or indifferent of one of God's poor, like old Rosie.

Well, you ask, how can it be made better? My answer is that there ought to be a radical change in the Board of Control of Public Institutions. I do not make any personal fight on the three men now in control. I make war on the whole system. As it is now, there are, in and about Boston, ten public institutions, occupied by thousands of men and women and children, carried on at an expense of nearly six hundred thousand dollars, entirely under the control of three commissioners. This is not wise. There ought to be a large advisory board made up of distinguished citizens. This should be composed of women as well as men. It is certainly a very short-sighted and thoughtless arrangement that, although there are in these institutions several hundred women and children, there is no woman who has any authorized interest in them. There is every reason why women should be on the Boards of Control of Public Institutions. The editor of the New York *Nation* says: "Whatever improvement there has been in the condition of Bellevue Hospital, for example, and of the hospitals of Blackwell's and Hart's Islands, during the past twenty years — and it is very great — has, as a rule, been due to women's initiative and labors."

The fact is, that everything that concerns health, education, and good morals occupies the minds of women more than it does the minds of most of their husbands and fathers; and in every department of municipal administration, where the conditions of the streets, of the sewers, of the hospitals and almshouses, and of the police, are in question, women have an equal interest with men, and in order to the public well-being and safety, ought to have an equal voice. I am sure that an advisory board of leading citizens, on which were three or four level-headed, humane women, would work the revolution that is needed in the treatment of Boston's paupers. Do not put this question aside. This is Boston's question, and you are a part of Boston. As some one sang in the Boston *Transcript* not long ago: —

> " Lazarus lies at your gate!
>   O proud and prosperous city,
> How long will you let him wait?
>   Listen and look; have pity.
>
> Dives, oh, cannot you hear,
>   For the music and dance of your high land,
> The moaning of misery drear
>   That comes from the desolate island?
>
> Finest of linen you wear;
>   Comrades in luxury you cherish,
> Sumptuous daily you fare.
>   What of your neighbors who perish?

When you would heighten your cheer
   By a contrast that's very dramatic,
Fancy what scenes may appear
   In a certain dim hospital attic.

Swarming and sweltering, and scant
   Of air, — foul to soul as to senses, —
Where he that is guilty of Want
   Meets a doom fit for graver offences.

Worn-out, the pauper nurse sleeps;
   The sufferer, forsaken, is crying
With no one to moisten his lips, —
   No one to mark that he's dying.

Who should hear the *catch* in his breath
   'Mid the coughs, curses, ravings, resounding
Through the ward o'er the bed of his death,
   From the close-crowded pallets surrounding?

And picture the scenes, to come
   Perhaps, of another sorrow
Nearer your stately home,—
   That you will not have to borrow;

When hushed is all merry din,
   And your smiling guests have vanished;
When your flowers come blooming in,
   To be glanced at once and banished;

When vain are all the crafts
   That Mammon serve, and never
Your costliest, coolest draughts
   Can quench the fire of your fever;

When your street is red with tan,
   And your oft-pulled door-bell muffled,
That the peace of a dying man
   By no faintest sound be ruffled;

When love, to give you rest,
   Doth toil with soothings fruitless;
And skill has done its best,
   And the town's best skill is bootless;

When the chaises leave the place,
   And the helpless, poor patrician
Lies looking up in the face
   Of only the Great Physician, —

God grant it with joy may be
   That you hear, 'What you did toward others
Ye have done it unto Me,
   In the least of those My brothers!'

Lazarus lies at your gate;
   Our kindly dear old city,
Let him no longer wait;
   Open the doors of your pity!"

XI

COMMENT ON "OUR BROTHERS AND SISTERS, THE BOSTON PAUPERS"

"There is no caste in blood,
Which runneth of one hue, nor caste in tears,
Which trickled salt with all."

XI

COMMENT ON "OUR BROTHERS AND SISTERS, THE BOSTON PAUPERS"

MRS. ALICE N. LINCOLN, who has given a large amount of time and painstaking interest to the treatment of the paupers, and who deserves more credit than any one else for the present hopeful campaign in their behalf, writes as follows in the *Boston Transcript* of August 28: —

"Those of your readers who were kind enough to follow in your columns, last winter, the articles for which you courteously made space there concerning the poor of Boston, will, I think, be interested to know what has since been done for the islands, and why so much controversy is aroused by the sermon of Dr. Banks on the paupers.

"Early in the spring two new commissioners were appointed. It was hoped that this change in the board would bring about good results, but, in point of fact, matters remained much the same. The appropriation for a new hospital, though made months ago, was not acted upon until this week, when bids for the building were opened.

WOMEN'S HOSPITAL WARD AT LONG ISLAND.[1]

"On August 5 I had the honor to lay before the commissioners eight requests on behalf of the inmates of the island, as follows: —

"1. More occupation for the able-bodied.

"2. More comfortable chairs for the aged women, who are obliged to rise at 5.30 A.M., and

[1] This is the best hospital ward on the two islands. Screen shown on the right, behind which is a dying woman.

are not allowed to lie down without permission.

"3. More benches out of doors for the benefit of the inmates.

"4. A separate room for the dying (it having been urged by both the physician and superintendent that the cries of dying patients often disturbed a whole ward for several nights).

"5. More privacy for women in bathing (and it will, perhaps, shock your readers, as it did the writer, that one of the commissioners affirmed and repeated that he did not consider this necessary).

"6. Another nurse at Long Island, where Miss O'Brian has charge of fifty-two sick women and where there is no bath-room.

"7. Another nurse at the Main Institution Building on Rainsford Island, where the laundry-matron has charge of forty-two sick women in addition to her other duties, and with no assistance except what is given her by inmates.

"8. A new matron for the hospital. My reason for making this last request is that I believe the present matron to be inefficient.

She has had no previous hospital training to fit her for her duties, and certainly the hospital and its patients, when I last saw them, bore evidences of neglect. The beds were not clean, and the patients showed a lack of personal cleanliness and care. When I first visited the hospital the floors were dirty and the closets were unwashed, but there has been an improvement in those respects. I was present when dinner was served to thirty patients in one ward — or, indeed, to seventy inmates of the hospital — and the matron took no charge of the food, which was put before the patients in a most uninviting manner — a great contrast to the neat wooden trays which are in use at Tewksbury. Moreover, I discerned a want of interest in the patients, to which the matron herself bore testimony when she said that she never washed a wound, and was engaged as a matron — not as a nurse.

"These, then, were the grounds upon which I asked for the appointment of another nurse or matron, and fortunately one has applied for the position entirely without my knowledge or solicitation. One of the commissioners doubted whether a trained hospital emergency nurse could be found to go to the islands; but this offer seems to set that question at rest, and it is to be hoped her application may be considered favorably.

"I also had the honor to lay before the commissioners the report of one of my former tenants, who was an inmate of Rainsford Island a little more than a year ago.

"She was a young woman who went down there because of a lump in her breast, taking her baby with her. But for the baby she would have been admitted to the City Hospital; but she did not like to leave her child, and her husband, who was absent, was unable to care for it. Consequently, she became for the time an inmate of the Rainsford Island Hospital.

"She complained first of the indignity of having to strip in the presence of others, no screen or curtain being provided as a shelter to the necessary bath, which is the first step on entrance to an institution.

"During her stay of three weeks she had no towel given to her, and only one clean sheet was furnished.

"She was expected to cook all the food for her baby, and to make and clean her own bed, although she was partly incapacitated by the lump in her breast, which affected one arm.

"The food was very poor and unsatisfactory; and when she complained that the porridge was sour, the matron told her if she did not like it she could leave it.

"Worse than all, her baby fell ill on a Wednesday; she could obtain no medicine for it until Sunday (though she asked for it repeatedly), and on Monday the baby died.

"The mother left the institution the next day. She speaks in the highest terms of the physician in charge and of the assistant, Miss McDonald, at Rainsford Island; but she says the matron never did anything for her and was not with her when the baby died; also, that the milk and other food ordered for the patients is often not received by them. And in this respect her statement is corroborated by the remarks of another woman, also my tenant, who was an inmate of Long Island when it was first opened for women several years ago. This woman told me, with bated breath, that the food was miserable — it was killing her; and, indeed, she died soon after, though I think grief hastened her end.

GETTING A BREATH OF FRESH AIR.

"It is because I have seen these people in their own homes that I feel such sympathy for them as paupers. They have known the comfort and independence of their own surroundings, and if by reason of old age or sickness — through no fault of their own — they become paupers, they should at least be treated with due consideration and nursed with all tenderness. I am entering no plea for the lazy and idle and intemperate class who seek the refuge of an almshouse, and for whom, as Dr. Banks says, the work-house is the proper place; but I do say that old or sick people, even if paupers, are entitled to the very best care. We do not begrudge it to them in our City Hospital or our State almshouse; therefore, why is it too much to require it of the city of Boston's pauper hospitals?

"No wonder that an attack such as has been made by Dr. Banks meets with violent opposition and denial. He is attacking institutions whose officials depend for their bread and butter on the positions which they fill. But Dr. Banks and I have no 'axe to grind,' and he is only stating the truth when he says that the pauper institutions at Rainsford Island are overcrowded (so overcrowded that nearly fifty old women sleep in a close and stifling attic, under the roof), and that the fare, especially for the old and sick, is not what it should be."

The *Boston Herald* of August 30 begins an exhaustive article, more than five columns long, by saying: —

"For some time there has been an earnest and vigorous agitation going on regarding the management and condition of Boston's pauper institutions at Long and Rainsford Islands. Heretofore this agitation has been out of the sight of the general public, with the exception of a few letters which have appeared from time to time in the papers; consequently, the sermon of Rev. Louis Albert Banks last Sunday on the subject came like a revelation to many.

"The *Herald* had been making a thorough investigation of the charges brought, previous to Mr. Banks' utterances, and this has been continued up to the present time, in order that the people of Boston may know accurately and to the fullest the precise condition of its pauper institutions and their inmates. As a result of that investigation, it may be boldly said that the criticisms which have been made public do not give an adequate idea of the disgraceful condition in which the institutions are at present, nor the treatment which the paupers receive and under which they exist rather than live.

"This statement is a strong one, but it can be borne out by facts which are indisputable."

In the course of this long article, which fully sustains all statements set forth in my discourse, the *Herald* reporter, commenting on the crowded condition of the buildings on Rainsford Island, says:—

"It is in the main building at Rainsford that the greatest lack of even decent surroundings prevails, and where the condition of the inmates is the worst. Here the fault seems to lie not only with the commissioners, but with the matrons in charge, for there is no system discernible in the housekeeping arrangements whatever. The infirmary is occupied by those women who are not able to get about; and the rooms composing that part of the building are pleasant and airy of themselves, but they are spoiled by their keeping. There is no classification of inmates, and old and young are all together, as well as the vicious and the unfortunate.

"Another classification which might be made was suggested by the presence of two women who were so unfortunate as to be afflicted in such a manner that the whole air of the room was contaminated on their account. This was through no fault of their own, and they should not be made to suffer for it; but it seems hardly fair that all the other women should be compelled to breathe the air made foul by their presence. Add to this detriment to health and decent living the bad sanitary arrangements, and the result is, indeed, open to criticism.

" This building is so old and antiquated that it originally had no place provided inside for water-closets and bath-rooms. In putting these in they were built directly in the corners of the rooms; and these corners were then partitioned off, but for some unknown reason the partitions were not continued up to the ceilings, the result being that the closets were practically left in the room and a screen put around. Owing to the fact that there is no water on the island, it all being brought in tanks by steamer, there is not that abundance used in flushing out the bowls which otherwise might be the case, and which would go so far toward removing the horrible odor which is so prevalent in every part of the building. Aside from the discomfort in being obliged to smell this odor continually, the danger to the health of the inmates is a serious thing.

"Throughout the wards in this building there is considerable overcrowding, although not to the extent that is to be seen in another part. The beds are all cared for by the women themselves, and conversation with the matron showed that there was a regular time for changing the bed linen, although that time was not the same in any two rooms, and the writer, after continued questioning and asking for explanation, failed to discover that there was any regularity whatever about it.

"A few beds were taken at random and stripped to see their condition. Invariably the sheets were dirty, very dirty; but this was explained by one of the inmates who was in charge of this ward by the statement that it was time they were changed, according to their usual practice, but for some reason, not given, it had not been done this week. On nearly all the sheets were plainly seen the marks of dead bed-bugs and other vermin, some of it dried on and looking as though it had been there for a long time.

"It is in the attic of the main building, how-

ATTIC AT RAINSFORD ISLAND.

ever, that one should go to realize some of Dickens' pictures of pauper life, for there is a picture here that needs no exaggeration to make it appear on a par with those in fiction.

[1] Cut shows one wing. Another crosses it at right angles and is partly occupied. Thirty women occupy this room, allowing about 320 cubic feet of air-space per person. The only ventilation is through windows jutting out on the roof, each one being 2 feet 10 inches by 4 feet 8 inches in size.

In this attic live the older women, and they pass their sleeping hours and many of their waking ones under the eaves of this old house.

" Throughout this attic the peak is so low that it can be touched by the hand of a man of ordinary height while standing, and the roof pitches until it comes to within two feet of the floor. Under the eaves here are placed the beds of these old women, their heads close under the roof, and extending in a line down the length of the building.

" The width of this attic is eighteen feet, and its length is that of the building; but it is divided up into several apartments. In one of these apartments were thirty beds, all occupied at night. The total air-space of this room allowed about three hundred and twenty cubic feet to each person, where a thousand are considered necessary with good ventilation, according to Mr. Commissioner Newell. The only light and ventilation that this attic gets is through a few small windows let into the roof, not large enough to furnish ventilation for rooms which are not overcrowded, and certainly not large enough to purify rooms where the air is made foul by being breathed by at least three times too many persons.

"Moreover, these old women are required to rise every morning at 5.30 o'clock, and are compelled to remain up until 8 o'clock in the evening. They are not allowed to lie down during the day without a special permit from the doctor, as, they say, it would cause disorder. This permit he says he is always willing to grant, but they seldom come for it. This seems perfectly natural, as one hardly can expect that the old women would take pains to hunt up the doctor every time they wanted to take a short nap.

"Not only are they not allowed to lie down for a nap without this special permit, but comfortable chairs are not furnished them. By each bed is a single ordinary wooden chair of the cheapest kind, and this is allotted to the one occupying the bed. Now and then a rocking-chair may be seen, but they are few and far between.

"Some time ago a benevolent and kind-hearted lady visiting the island was struck with this lack of comfort, and sent to the institution a number of rocking-chairs for use in the old women's ward. They arrived on July 16, but an active search for them failed to disclose their whereabouts. It was plain that the women for

MARINERS' HOME.

whom they were intended were not getting the benefit of them, and inquiry was made. Nobody seemed to know where they were. Several believed that something of the kind had been sent down, but knew nothing more,

Finally, after an energetic search by Dr. Harkins, the chairs were discovered in a storehouse, or paint-shop, where they had been put when they landed on the wharf so long ago. Two days later these chairs had been taken out and placed in the wards, and there were two hundred women eager for the six comfortable rockers.

"Another criticism which might be made is that the paupers are provided with no regular religious service. At Deer Island there is a paid chaplain, and although his duties do not call him to the almshouse, he sometimes goes over. There is a large room called the chapel, and here religious services are held when there is any one to lead them. A Catholic priest goes down twice a week to minister to the wants of the Catholics, who are in the majority; something like ninety-five per cent being of that persuasion. The fact remains, however, that the city of Boston does not give its paupers the benefit of any religious service or guidance. As was said by one lady on hearing the facts: 'In the eyes of the city it is a greater crime to be a pauper than a criminal.'"

Rev. Dr. Frederick B. Allen, of the Episcopal City Mission of Boston, writing in the *Herald* of August 31, says: —

"In the management of human beings, especially the aged, the infirm, the insane, and the sick, there is needed a wise and tender consideration which sheer business management is apt to miss.

"The sociological problems of pauperism and crime, the study of successful methods in other cities and other lands, the deep sense of the sacredness of our humanity, even in its weakest and most unfortunate members, — these make their demand for the aid of men and women to whom these questions of human life and death are at least as controlling as the reduction of the city tax rate.

"Were there any such board of advisers to do in our city institutions what the State Charities Aid Society has done for New York State, we should not have been confronted, as we now are, with poorly planned, inadequate, and badly managed buildings, lack of discrimination in those permitted to occupy them, insufficient and untrained nurses for the sick, lack of proper ventilation and food, and everywhere the absence of devoted personal, human, moral oversight and control.

"I second most positively Dr. Banks' assertion that 'an advisory board of leading citizens, on which are three or four level-headed and humane women, would work the revolution that is needed in the treatment of " our brothers and sisters, the Boston paupers." ' "

XII

THE GOLD GOD OF MODERN SOCIETY

"When wealth no more shall rest in mounded heaps,
But smit with freer light shall slowly melt
In many streams to fatten lower lands,
And light shall spread, and man be liker man
Thro' all the seasons of the golden year."

XII

THE GOLD GOD OF MODERN SOCIETY

NO one who is in touch with the throbbing life of this time can fail to perceive that this is an age peculiarly given up to the worship of Mammon. The literature of our day bears certain evidence of this fact. *Scribner's Magazine* of last year contained, under the title of "Jerry," a painfully realistic and comprehensive story, dealing with the debauch of a noble character by the fascination of gold. Jerry belonged to the "poor white trash" of the Cumberland Mountains, and on the death of his mother, being cruelly treated at home, he ran away to the West. After many wanderings, the little wayfarer, tired out and almost dead, fell into the hands of a quaint old miner who was digging and hoarding up gold in his cabin in the Northwestern Mountains. In the midst of this wild region, educated by a kind-hearted physician, Jerry grew up to be a young man of peculiarly noble and heroic character. He remembered with painful distinctness that he belonged to the poorest of the common people, and the ambition of his life was to uplift his own class.

The fearful tragedy of the story begins when the miserly old miner — who, all the time unknown to Jerry, is hoarding up gold for his young ward — discovers, to his great astonishment, that gold has no fascination for this strange young man, and fears that with his lofty ideals all his toil for him will be in vain and unappreciated. So the shrewd old man plans to send him to the East, where his eyes may be dazzled with the brilliancy of fashionable life, and where may be revealed to him the power gold gives to its possessor. Sitting in his old log cabin on the mountain side, the old miner would rub his hands back on his stubbly gray hair and reason with himself: "If Jerry only knew gold; if Jerry could only see what gold could get, could only spend gold; then he would be willing to take all he could get and never ask where it came from." So the old miner determined that "Jerry must learn to spend money, must learn to love it, and then all will go well." And then the story goes on to tell of the deterioration of this noble young soul — how that gradually he becomes dominated with the passion for gold, until he is not only willing to work for it, but murder for it, if only he may have gold and the power that it brings.

In another field Mr. Charles Dudley Warner gives us the same warning, in his story of "A Little Journey in the World." In this Mr. Warner tells us of one of the sweetest and purest of young women, who has the highest ideals, and whose standards of morality are of the noblest, who is married to an unprincipled young speculator on Wall Street, New York; and under the influence of her husband, and the society into which she is drawn by his business relations, in which he gathers millions of money, all her holy and lofty ideals are overthrown, and she becomes simply a material, worldly woman. This is the way he reasons about it: "But we, I say, who loved her, and knew so well the noble possibilities of her royal nature, under circumstances favorable to its development, felt more and more her departure from her own ideals. Her life in its spreading prosperity seemed more and more shallow. I do not say she was heartless; I do not say she was uncharitable; I do not say that in all the externals of worldly and religious observance she was wanting; I do not say that the more she was assimilated to the serenely worldly nature of her husband, she did not love him, or that she was unlovely in the worldliness that ingulfed her and bore her onward. I do not know that there is anything singular in her history. But the pain of it to us was in the certainty — and it seemed so near — that in the decay of her higher life, in the hardening process of a material existence, in the transfer of all her interest to the trivial and sensuous gratifications — time, mind, heart, ambition, all fixed on them — we should never regain our Margaret. What I saw in a vision of her future was a *dead soul* — a beautiful woman in all the success of envied prosperity, with a dead soul."

If we turn away from these revelations of

the worm at the heart of our social life, that are made fascinating by the art in which they are clothed, to the rude happenings of every-day observation, the same danger is everywhere

CHILDREN PLAYING IN COPP'S HILL BURYING GROUND.

apparent. The associated press despatches from San José, Cal., a few weeks since, bore this burden: "One of the best-known men in California died yesterday in a squalid hut on Colfax Street. He was Prof. Herman Kottinger, who at one time was the leading violinist on the Pacific Coast, and well known as a writer of prose and poetry, of 'A World's History,' and also of text-books on free thought. He was worth hundreds of thousands of dollars, acquired by a lifetime of miserly frugality. At the time of his death sixteen hundred dollars in gold coin was found secreted in his bed. But one child, William Kottinger, a farmer, was present at the death. When the old man in his death-throes raised himself up in bed, the son rushed to his side. His father, mistaking the act, with a frenzied yell waved him back, and clutching at the bedclothes, pulled them back, disclosing to view the gold. He made a grab at it with both hands, and with the bright pieces in his fingers fell back with a gasp and expired.

"Prof. Kottinger was once a doctor in Heidelberg University, and was ninety years old. He was so wasted by hunger that his body weighed less than forty pounds, and was in a disgusting condition. His bed and clothes were reeking with filth. Over the head of the bed hung a violin of great value. So miserly was the old professor that fifteen years ago he drove his wife and all his children from home, saying that it cost too much to feed and clothe them. From that day until yesterday, when the end was approaching, not one of his relatives had come near him. Two big fierce Danish mastiffs, half starved, have for years been the old man's only companions, and they guarded the shanty so well that not even a tax-collector could approach. They had to be killed yesterday before the undertaker could get into the house. When it was learned that Kottinger was dead, a number of his relatives hastened to his hut. There has been a shameful neglect of the dead shown, and indecent haste in ransacking the place in search of the gold and other treasures known to be hidden."

All these show the destructive power of gold upon its worshippers. But these are by no means the only victims of this worship of the gold god. For every one who is hoarding up his millions, and who is dominated by the love of gold for its very shine and glitter, there are hundreds and thousands who are toiling for insufficient wages, and are suffering in poverty and want, that this lordly worshipper may pay his devotions to the money god.

If some of these money kings who have made their millions by the oppression of the poor, in mines, and mills, and factories, were suddenly called to face the bones of the dead

DIGGING IN THE ASH-BARRELS IN WINTER.

who have gone to their graves from weary, unrequited slavery, in order for their financial triumph, they would stand back aghast at the price of their own success.

It is this worship of the gold god which is at

the bottom of all the wrongs which have been pointed out in this series of discourses. The wealthy merchant who pays the poor widow one cent apiece for making white aprons, and by his avarice and his lust induces the young women who sell them to eke out their scanty wages by the sale of their honor, is a worshipper of the gold god. The sweater who parcels out his work through the miserable tenement houses, grinding the face of the poor to the very last degree possible with physical existence, — indeed, many times beyond the possibility of existence, except when helped by charity, — is an obsequious devotee at the altar of Mammon. The chattel-mortgage shark, who watches all the necessities of the poor as anxiously as ever a hawk watched over a helpless or crippled bird, and the liquor-seller, who fills his coffers by a traffic which injures and destroys the health, the intelligence, and the morality of all the people whom he can draw into his net, investing all his cunning in methods to entrap the unwary, and gloating over the increasing appetite and the devilish passion for strong drink in his victims, are only brothers to the others who gather to pay their devotions to the god of gold.

If we do not approve these worshippers, what shall we say of ourselves for permitting this state

FOUR SHINERS.

of things to come to pass? It is inconsistent to condemn the liquor-seller and honor the city which licenses him to do his damnable work. It is impossible to condemn the sweater and retain your respect for the public which permits him to carry on his nefarious business. The spirit of avarice is in the very air, until society has been poisoned by its breath. Dr. Howard Crosby, writing in the *Forum* a few years since, says: " The healthiest form of human society is where the many are equally independent in their management of their affairs, where professions and trades are represented by individual thinking minds, and where those engaged in any one branch of industry stand on a level with one another. This condition of things promotes invention, activity, interest, manliness, and good citizenship. Now the gold-hunt system is directly antagonistic to all this. It seeks to destroy the many independent tradesmen, and to make them servants in a gigantic monopoly. The happy homes of freemen become the pinched quarters of serfs. The lords of trade have their hundreds and thousands of humble subordinates over whom they rule, often with a rod of iron. They may be turned away from work and wages at any moment, by any whim of the selfish employer. Hence, through fear of this, they lose their manhood, and dare not assert even a decision of their conscience. There is no more melancholy sight to my eyes than that which I often see nowadays — the former happy possessor of a shop or store, who has lived comfortably and with the true nobility of a citizen, and whose family have felt the dignity of the home, now made a clerk and drudge in a huge establishment that, by its relentless use of millions, has undermined and overthrown all the independent stores of a large district, while his family are thrust into the unsavory communism of a tenement house, and lose all the delicate refinements of a quiet home. It is easy to say that this is but the natural law of trade. So to devour men is the natural law of tigers. But this truth will not reconcile us to the process. If we are to stop men from stealing directly, we can stop them from stealing indirectly. If natural law works evil to the community, we are to make statute law, which will act as supernatural law, and control the offensive principle. Unless we wish our social equality destroyed, and a system of practical serfdom to take its place, we must put a limit to the acts of greed, and so preserve the independence of our citizens."

THE GOLD GOD OF MODERN SOCIETY 317

Every thoughtful observer of the "signs of the times" knows that the deepest problem of our age is the amicable solution of the struggle between labor and capital. Some of

SOUTH BOSTON RAG-PICKERS.

the ablest work done in literature, in our time, has been produced out of an earnest desire to abolish the more recent types of this white slavery, which has, in one form or another, threatened the masses since the days of old John Ball of early England. Perhaps the strongest portrayal, yet, of many phases of the question, especially those relating to the city, may be found in Mr. Howells' story, "A Hazard of New Fortunes." For the country, if one really wants to see what is behind the great upheaval in the West, which has its outward manifestation in the Farmers' Alliance, he only needs to read Mr. Hamlin Garland's "Main Travelled Roads."

In the meantime most of us are asking, "What is the way out?" As for myself, I confess to being only a student. I have no word of sneer or scoff for any man's honest thinking, who is sincerely trying to uplift his brothers and sisters; and yet I must say that, as yet, I have not been able to become a disciple of any of the new systems that have been presented. I feel something like the man who says, "There are good things to be said in praise of Socialism or Nationalism, as compared with the crushing and wearing methods of competition; but what the world is waiting for is the thinker who shall either show us how to reconcile the new system with human liberty, or else convince us that we can do without liberty." In the meantime I believe in God, in His wise purpose in the creation of the world, in His providential care over it, and that under His grace there shall come the triumph of righteousness in it. I believe in Jesus Christ. To my mind, Christianity stands to-day very much as it did nearly two thousand years ago, when Jesus hung upon the cross between two thieves. The anarchy which, atheistic and reckless, would destroy all law and all property, is one of the thieves, and the devotee of the gold god of our time, who clutches his money-bags and says, "I have a right to get all the money I can, and do with it what I please," is the other thief. Christianity stands between them; her mission is to change them both, and bring them with a regenerated purpose into brotherhood and fellowship.

George Macdonald says: "The world will change only as the heart of man changes. Growing intellect, growing civilization, will heal man's wounds only to cause the deeper ill to break out afresh in new forms, nor can they satisfy one longing of the human soul. Its desires are deeper than that soul itself, whence it groans with the groanings that cannot be uttered. As much in times of civilization as in those of barbarity, the soul needs an external presence to make its life good to it." The Christianity of to-day must set itself, as did Jesus, to make men brothers, by bringing them to a recognition of the fact that they are all alike the children of one God and Father over all. Such a Christianity will necessarily be at war with the gold god of our time. The clear-cut declaration of Jesus, "Ye cannot serve God and Mammon," is as true now as when He uttered it. I do not remember to have seen this issue put as clearly anywhere else as by Henry D. Lloyd in an article in the *North American Review* entitled, "The New Conscience." He says: Let us listen while a delegation from the Money-power remonstrates with the New Conscience for its unreasonable sentiments and ideas. Here they come, one by one, and range themselves about. First speaks —

THE MERCHANT PRINCE: I have a right to buy where I can buy cheapest.

CONSCIENCE: See these little stunted, hollow-eyed girls coming out of that factory.

LAWYER: Wages are settled by contract.

CONSCIENCE: Where can I find white-haired workingmen?

CAPITALIST: Every man has a right to do what he will with his own.

CONSCIENCE: What is the price of a senatorship to-day?

STATISTICIAN: Never were food, fuel, and clothing so cheap.

CONSCIENCE: Little Mary Mitchell works in Waterbury's ropeworks five days a week from six in the evening till six in the morning.

RAILROAD KING: Every man makes his own career. I was a workingman myself twenty years ago, and now I keep a carriage, a butler, and several judges and legislators, in four States, and —

CONSCIENCE: That tired-looking man is a railway conductor of a company owned by half a dozen men worth three hundred millions of dollars, which is not enough for them, so they squeeze a few more dollars a month out of him by making him, on every alternate trip, do twenty-eight and a half hours' work without sleep.

BANKER: Our wealth is increasing one billion dollars a year. We have boards of trades, the best railroads in the world, and packing-houses that can kill ten thousand hogs.

CONSCIENCE: The sickening stench, the blistered air, the foul sights of the tenements, and the motherhood and the childhood choking there.

CONSERVATIVE: This is the best government in the world. America is good enough for me.

CONSCIENCE: Listen to that "tramp, tramp, tramp" of a million of men out of work.

MANUFACTURER: Without this system of industry the subjugation of North America to civilization would have been impossible; we could never have shown the world the magnificent spectacle of —

CONSCIENCE: There is a little boy standing ten hours a day up to his ankles in the water in a coal-mine.

COAL MONOPOLIST: I have a statistician who can prove — he can prove anything — that the workingman is a great deal better off than he ever was, that he makes more than I do, that small incomes are increasing and large ones decreasing, that there is no involuntary poverty, and that the workingmen could live on twenty-five cents each a day and buy up the United States with their savings, and —

CONSCIENCE: How long shall it be cheaper to run over workingmen and women at the railroad crossings in the cities than to put up gates?

CLERGYMAN: The poor we are to have with us always.

CONSCIENCE: That sewing-woman you see pawning her shawl has lived this winter with her two children in a room without fire. Are you wearing one of the shirts she finished?

STATESMAN: The workingman has the ballot and the newspapers. He is a free citizen.

CONSCIENCE: As the nights grow colder see how the number of girls on the street increases.

It is this new conscience, the conscience of Jesus Christ, that appraises a hungry child to be of more value than ten thousand palaces, that must animate and dominate the church that is called by His name, in its war against the gold god of modern society.

You may find this conscience throbbing in

Ella Wheeler Wilcox's plea for "Justice, not Charity."

> " All hail the dawn of a new day breaking,
>   When a strong armed nation shall take away
>   The weary burden from backs that are aching
>   With maximum work and minimum pay.
>
>   When no man is honored who hoards his millions,
>   When no man feasts on another's toil,
>   And God's poor, suffering, starving billions
>   Shall share His riches of sun and soil.
>
>   There is gold for all in the world's broad bosom,
>   There is food for all in the world's great store;
>   Enough is provided if rightly divided,
>   Let each man take what he needs — no more.
>
>   Shame on the miser with unused riches,
>   Who robs the toiler to swell his hoard,
>   Who beats down the wage of the digger of ditches,
>   And steals the bread from the poor man's board!
>
>   Shame on the owner of mines whose cruel
>   And selfish measures have brought him wealth!
>   While the ragged wretches who dig his fuel
>   Are robbed of comfort, and hope, and health.
>
>   Shame on the ruler who rides in his carriage,
>   Bought by the labor of half-paid men —
>   Men who are shut out of home and marriage,
>   And are herded like sheep in a hovel pen."

There must be no doubt about the attitude of the church in a time like this. Against the gold god and all his oppressions the Christian Church must stand with an unflinching front. Our God is the same who spoke through the voice of Amos of old, saying, "Hear this, oh ye that swallow up the needy, even to make the poor of the land to fail, saying, When will the new moon be gone, that we may sell corn? And the sabbath, that we may set forth wheat, making the ephah small, and the shekel great, and falsifying the balances by deceit? That we may buy the poor for silver, and the needy for a pair of shoes; yea, and sell the refuse of the wheat?" Ah! how much that sounds like the things that are going on at the present time! Yet listen to the oath of the Almighty as He looks on such things: "The Lord hath sworn by the excellency of Jacob, Surely I will never forget any of their works. Shall not the land tremble for this, and every one mourn that dwelleth therein? . . . And it shall come to pass in that day, saith the Lord God, that I will cause the sun to go down at noon, and I will darken the earth in a clear day: and I will turn your feasts into mourning, and all your songs into lamentation; and I will bring up sackcloth upon all loins, and baldness upon every head; and I will make it as the mourning of an only son, and the end thereof as a bitter day."

It is the mission of our blessed Christianity to save the world from that bitter day by so changing and transforming it that it will no longer deserve bitterness, but peace, at the hand of God. Although I have felt compelled, in this series of discourses, to uncover many dark and loathsome places in our social system, yet I am no pessimist, and I do not despair. Jesus Christ, our Captain, saw "Satan fallen as lightning from heaven;" and when we are as devoted to God, and as thoroughly consecrated to our mission of curing the world's heartache as was He, we, too, shall live in sight of the same glorious triumph. When we are imbued with this faith, and exalted into fellowship with Him, we will not dare to say that the sweat-shop, or the neglected tenement house, or the noisome liquor saloon, is a necessary contingent of human life. And we will know that whatever is good enough to be true, may be and shall be true to the sons and daughters of

God. In that faith we shall be able to sing with the poet: —

> "'Tis coming up the steeps of time,
>   And this old world is growing brighter;
> We may not see its dawn sublime,
>   Yet high hopes make the heart throb lighter!
>
> We may be sleeping in the ground,
>   When it awakes the peoples' wonder;
> But we have felt it gathering round,
>   And heard its voice of living thunder;
>   Christ's reign, ah, yes, 'tis coming!
>
> Aye, it *must* come! the Tyrant's throne
>   Is crumbling, with men's hot tears rusted;
> The sword earth's mighty have leant upon
>   Is cankered, with men's hearts' blood crusted!
>
> Room! for the man of love make way!
>   Ye selfish great ones, pause no longer;
> Ye cannot stay the opening day,
>   The world rolls on, the light grows stronger —
>   The Master's advent's coming!"

www.ingramcontent.com/pod-product-compliance
Lightning Source LLC
Chambersburg PA
CBHW030729230426
43667CB00007B/651